I0634488

SLEEPING IN THE COURTYARD

More advance praise for *Sleeping in the Courtyard*

"As a Palestinian American writer, I have long searched for reflections of my own fragmented lineage—this anthology gave me that and more. *Sleeping in the Courtyard* is more than an anthology—it is a reclamation. At once fierce and tender, the collection defies monolithic portrayals of Kurdish identity and instead renders a chorus of nuance, complexity, and lived truth. From the ruins of Halabja to the rooftops of Baghdad, from the quiet defiance of translation to the unbreakable thread of community, this anthology is a testament to the power of writing as cultural survival—and as revolutionary act. Curated with deep care and transnational breadth, *Sleeping in the Courtyard* invites readers into a space of shared breath, radical empathy, and collective remembrance. It is a door flung open. A night under the stars. A home built from story. This is not just a collection—it's a homecoming, a collective heartbeat, a defiant archive of what refuses to be erased."

  —**Etaf Rum**, author of *Evil Eye*

"What a gift we have in this gorgeous and significant anthology of Kurdish writing, and what a sheer joy to read. Sharply and lovingly curated by Holly Mason Badra, this is a landmark collection of works from Kurdish writers representing a constellation of histories, positionalities, possibilities. The offerings here are astonishing in their beauty and inventiveness, framed by Mason Badra's keen and generous introduction. This book is a site for urgent collectivity, a welcoming home to Kurdish stories for Kurdish readers, and in its specificities, a window into the condition of being human. These vital words will stay with me."

  —**Lana Salah Barkawi**, executive and artistic director of Mizna

"*Sleeping in the Courtyard* moved me in ways I didn't expect. As a Kurdish woman, I felt at home in these pages. Each piece carries the weight of memory, exile, and identity, but also the beauty of our language, our stories, our resilience. This collection doesn't just speak to the Kurdish experience—it honours it. It's raw, lyrical, and necessary. I'm proud to see these voices brought together, and I know they'll stay with me for a long time. *Sleeping in the Courtyard* made me feel a sense of temporary refuge—a place that isn't quite home, but holds a moment of safety, of reflection—and it took me back to sleeping in the courtyard back home during hot summer months."

  —**Payzee Mahmod**, girl's and women's rights campaigner

"Again and again the word 'dreams' emerges from the works in this collection. What else do 40 million people with no nation, no statehood, no citizenship have? So much—they have the words on these pages, the images and evocations that bring to life something far, far bigger than country. *Sleeping in the Courtyard* is an important work in a time of border tensions, showing that it is not a country that keeps a people, but their imaginations, longings, and dreams."

  —**Laleh Khadivi**, author of *The Kurdish Trilogy*

SLEEPING IN THE COURTYARD

Contemporary Kurdish Writers in Diaspora

Edited by
HOLLY MASON BADRA

THE UNIVERSITY OF ARKANSAS PRESS
Fayetteville ✳ 2025

Copyright © 2025 by the University of Arkansas Press. All rights reserved. No part of this book should be used or reproduced in any manner without prior permission in writing from the University of Arkansas Press or as expressly permitted by law.

ISBN: 978-1-68226-273-3
eISBN: 978-1-61075-838-3

29 28 27 26 25 5 4 3 2 1

Designed by William Clift

Library of Congress Cataloging-in-Publication Data
Names: Mason Badra, Holly editor
Title: Sleeping in the courtyard : contemporary Kurdish writers in diaspora / edited by
     Holly Mason Badra.
Description: Fayetteville : The University of Arkansas Press, 2025.
Identifiers: LCCN 2024052280 (print) | LCCN 2024052281 (ebook) |
     ISBN 9781682262733 paperback | ISBN 9781610758383 ebook
Subjects: LCSH: English literature—Kurdish authors | Literature—Translations into
     English | Kurdish literature—Translations into English | Arabic literature—Kurdish
     authors | LCGFT: Short stories | Poetry
Classification: LCC PN6014 .S54 2025 (print) | LCC PN6014 (ebook) |
     DDC 820.8/08915970905—dc23/eng/20250428
LC record available at https://lccn.loc.gov/2024052280
LC ebook record available at https://lccn.loc.gov/2024052281

To everyone else who should be in this collection,
please reach out so we can all be in community together.

To everyone who made it possible for us to be here,
Zor Spas.

Contents

HERO KURDA

Introduction

Who Are the Kurds?

This is a question I've been asked throughout my life, growing up in the southern United States, when I mention being Kurdish. Or, I'll get, *what is a Kurd?* I would be lying if I said that I have always had the *best* answer—or the most accurate one. Growing up, I think I was unsure myself, in some ways, of my ancestry. *Are you Arab?* No! *Oh, you mean Turkish?* Not quite.

Kurds are hospitality embodied. They are the epitome of resilience, and often described as the world's largest stateless ethnic group—the largest group without an official nation. There are over forty million Kurds living globally—likely much more, given that census fails in this context, as in many others. Kurds lost their land and autonomy when the Ottoman Empire claimed Kurdish territories. Their homeland was partitioned following World War I; thus, Kurdistan on the map stretches across "modern day" Syria, Turkey, Iran, and Iraq. Any political attempts Kurds have made for a self-governing Kurdistan have been denied by the "dominant" powers. In a move toward autonomy, some Kurds are now using the geographical phrasing of "Southern Kurdistan" instead of "Iraqi Kurdistan," for example (and "Eastern Kurdistan" instead of "Iranian Kurdistan"; "Northern Kurdistan" instead of "the Kurdish Region of Turkey"; and "Western Kurdistan" instead of "Kurdish Syria").

The Kurds have endured countless forms of militarized displacement, cultural destruction, and mass genocide. Saddam Hussein's Anfal campaign destroyed over 3,000 Kurdish villages and buried over 100,000 Kurds in mass graves (a chemical attack on Halabja in Southern Kurdistan instantly killed 5,000 people). Kurds are still haunted by the Dersim massacre in Northern Kurdistan, where over 45,000 Kurds were killed by Turkish soldiers (in part depicted in Kazim Öz's film *Zer* [2017]). Sanandaj (in Eastern Kurdistan) is sometimes referred to as "Bloodshed City" because of the genocide of Kurds that took place there from 1980 to 1985. And currently, we still see relentless Turkish attacks in Rojava (Western Kurdistan), where women-led protection units fight for Kurdish liberation. My goal here is not to belabor the oppression and destruction, but to offer a sliver of context. This contextual background will give readers an understanding around some of the themes that emerge in the anthology. But it's not just about a deficit model or what we are "without" . . . there is great bounty, too. And this anthology is interested in that fullness, also.

Togetherness

The idea of this collection first came to me in October 2019 when Western media brought attention to Kurdish oppression through coverage of the Turkish military attacks on Kurds in Rojava (Western Kurdistan). News coverage of this event led to North American and English-reading writers asking where they could find Kurdish poetry and literature translated into English. I took on the task of spotlighting and sharing what was readily available online, but the fact was that, at that time, there was not a vast overflow of Kurdish literary work translated into English *and* readily accessible, especially compared to translations of other languages from the SWANA region (Southwest Asia and North Africa), like Arabic, Turkish, or Farsi/Persian. Moreover, much of the Kurdish translations available and the few anthologies in existence at that point predominately offered space to male writers. The availability of women and nonbinary Kurdish writers translated into English was minimal.

So I began researching, reaching out, and recruiting writers to the project, with a focus on contemporary female and nonbinary voices. Upon compilation, this anthology has become more than a collection of writing. It is an embodiment of community. It has become a vehicle for connectivity. It is a site of togetherness. Through the gift of connecting with Kurdish, Kurdish hyphenated, and Kurdish writers in diaspora, we have started to form pathways for conversation and community building. We have utilized social media, WhatsApp, and Zoom to get to know each other, to collaborate, and to discuss our shared and distinct realities. It is through the visibility of being together in public conversations that we have also grown in numbers. We are out there. We exist. But now we are coming together to support each other and grow our creative Kurdish family.

Another reality that this collection aims to address is the fact that Kurds (especially Kurdish women) have often been written about by others who are not necessarily Kurdish themselves. The outsiders' gaze interpreting Kurdish experiences and stories for their audiences is a long-standing tradition and still a current practice today. The ethos of this anthology is "nothing about us without us"—it felt important to those in this collection that this work showcasing Kurdish female and nonbinary voices was brought into the world by someone from within the community. It was a task I did not take lightly and approached with steady care, ethical considerations, and deep mindfulness.

Being Kurdish American, in *my* experience, means that I was born in the US to a Kurdish mother and a white-Southern-Nashville father. My mother was born in Kirkuk (Southern Kurdistan) and grew up in Baghdad. Her family escaped Saddam Hussein's regime in 1975 (yes, he was persecuting the Kurds and "running the show" even before he was *officially* in a presidential position of power). They fled, packing one suitcase for ten, going on horseback through the mountains, and coming to the United States as war refugees. What this means is that my experience as a Kurdish American was one of distance and displacement from Kurdistan. But it was also growing up around my Kurdish family; hearing them speak a mixture of Arabic, Sorani, and Kurmanji; hearing stories about their lives before they immigrated to the US; and hearing them laugh in the kitchen together as they prepared a feast of Kurdish foods. Even though there was a displacement from the land, there was an immersion in Kurdish culture. At a young age, I could recite the details of my family's journey to get here: hiding in caves, the bomb that didn't detonate, the steep and thin mountain paths. And, in awe, I have learned about their experiences as refugees building a new "home" in America. Through connecting with other Kurdish writers and reading their work, I have been able to see my family's stories reflected and crystalized. More than that, as a daughter of diaspora, I have started to see my own world and experiences reflected as a queer, Kurdish American woman spanning various colliding spaces. That reflection has been incredibly—and unexpectedly—nourishing. I didn't know how much I needed to talk with others who have similar intersecting identities. It's been life-altering to be reflected in these ways, to be so understood. Connecting with other Kurdish writers and artists in this process has been uplifting and heart-healing—and I know I am not alone in those sentiments.

As children, my mom and her siblings not only learned both Arabic and Kurdish but also learned (sometimes the hard way) where they could or couldn't speak each language. Regrettably, I do not speak Kurdish fluently. This is also the case for many Kurds though, due to language oppression, suppression, and criminalization—intentional linguicide. This shows up in Kurdish and Kurdish diaspora writing. I say all this to point to the importance of collections like this not only as a way to showcase Kurdish stories but also to give space to Kurdish writing in translation. For diasporic Kurds who read in the English language, like myself, it's been electric to be able to read Kurdish stories, essays, and poetry thanks to the art of translation. I am grateful to the translators who are doing this difficult work. These translations offer a window . . . or more like a door to walk through, an entryway.

Most translations in this anthology are from Kurdish—and mostly from the Sorani dialect. There are many Kurdish dialects—to name a few: Kurmanji, Sorani, Gorani, Zazaki, Badini. However, it is important to note that linguicide has often made it impossible, if not criminal, for Kurds to learn Kurdish. To be clear, we still see this today. In January 2022, for example, Zahra Mohammadi was sentenced to five to ten years in prison for teaching the Kurdish language and literature to her students in Eastern Kurdistan (the Kurdish region of Iran). So, it is important to recognize that not all Kurds speak Kurdish and that this is deeply rooted in systemic oppression tactics to divide and conquer. When you cut off a group's ability to communicate in their mother tongue, you take away their capacity for connectivity. You take away their ability to share and preserve culture, to thrive. Or at least you attempt to. However, the Kurds remain resilient. Even in the face of these intentions to fracture, Kurds have remained some of the most tight-knit, friendly, warm, and welcoming people. We want to feed you. We want to hold your babies. We want to make sure you have what you need to be comfortable. A Kurd will give you the shirt off their back if you say you like it.

Given the fractured linguistic context described above, the other translations in the book are from Kurdish writers who do not write in Kurdish but rather are writing in Arabic, Turkish, Persian, or even Swedish. This was important to me to be as inclusive as possible in the collection and to recognize this complex web of physical and lingual displacement. Much of the writing in the book was originally written in English, but for the work that was translated into English, in reaching toward a decolonial praxis, it was important to me and the translators to find a publisher that would include the original Kurdish dialects to honor the Kurdish language, to recognize this history of linguicide, and to push against oppressive attempts to strip away Kurdish language.

My goal in this work was to be as expansive as possible in my approach and as transnational as possible in representation. We have in the book writers from and living in various parts of the world: Australia, the UK, Norway, Kurdistan, Iran, Iraq, Turkey, Syria, Jordan, France, Sweden, Greece, Germany, Austria, the US, and beyond. It was important to me that the writers included in the anthology also represent varied intersectional identities. The book had to be an open space for writers who also identify as queer and nonbinary; who are situated within various religious groups and belief systems; and/or who see themselves within the disability community.

At the university where I work, I am the faculty advisor for the Kurdish Student Organization. A few years ago, I asked the KSO's president, Ala, what she wanted the group to accomplish. She said, among other things, that she wanted people to know that "we aren't just sitting around eating dolma all the time." We all laughed. What Ala was getting at is what I hope this anthology will also achieve. A breaking of monolithic ideologies about Kurds . . . or, an opening. To enhance understanding around the varied lives and experiences of Kurds globally.

This collection resists confinement. This collection resists the appropriation of Kurdish cultural production. This collection resists the idea that Kurds are victims to be rescued by Western saviorism. It was important to me that the writing in this book moves beyond stereotypes. Yes, much of the writing, no doubt, conveys struggle—this is the reality, and especially related to the intersectionality of being a Kurdish woman. With these themes represented, I also wanted to offer a range of poems, stories, and essays that go beyond what some audiences *may* think of when they think of the Kurds. The writing in this book showcases a variety of representations, voices, points of view, identities, intersectional experiences, geographical contexts, as well as a range of styles and genres.

Some themes will quickly rise to the surface as you make your way through these pages: discovery, familial complexities, cultural suppression and exploration, gender-based violence and oppression, displacement, memory, resistance, and resilience. Beyond those common threads, there's also: strong female friendships (often like sisterhood), community, motherhood, parenthood, isolation, loss, female empowerment, sexuality, desire, love, bodily autonomy, immigration, exile, questions of "home," technology, music, art, legacy, lineage, ancestral meditations, complex and hyphenated identities, anger, fear, pursuit of education, familial struggles, familial bonds, sibling care, mental health, politics and political engagement, social critiques, feminist ideologies, travel, rootedness, fragmentation, epiphany, state violence, military occupation, genocide, lies, truths, artifacts, inheritance, food and feast, autumn foliage, summer heat, winter's breath, spring's perfume, dreams, magic, barriers, boundaries, war, liberation, rituals, intergenerational trauma, and intergenerational joy.

I considered how the works would speak to each other. How they might be in conversation, make conversation. What does it mean to have the protagonist in one essay desperate to go to school and then a few pages later have a nonfiction piece where a daughter interviews her mother on the college campus where they both graduated years apart? What happens when we read a poem that contemplates brutal isolation as an exiled writer and later land on a nonfiction essay that describes poetry as a shield from brutal systems? How do we process the delight of a grandmother reading tea leaves with her granddaughter in one poem ("honey-drenched, rose-scented, / stories run through my mind like sepia") closely followed by writing from another poet unpacking a tender moment of grandmother and grandchild meeting and embracing for the first time postwar ("if they were tears of joy / or of grief for the loss of my brother / who carried the same name")? A character in a novel excerpt struggles to look through old photographs (memory, a fickle friend), while in another the protagonist questions her work as a photographer. One writer marvels at the transcendent beauty of blue while another cannot unsee the white snow of genocide. One story reveals a forbidden relationship and another zooms in on a relationship unraveling. The works begin to speak to each other in interesting ways.

Sleeping in the Courtyard is really dedicated to *all* writers in exile. Many of the women in this book are writers in exile. They are exiled writers simply for being women *and* being writers (the two coexisting at once poses a threat). The fact that the intersecting identity as a Kurdish woman daring to write often means risking one's safety—simply for writing creatively—also proves that there must inherently be power in writing, if these women are seen as a threat just for doing it. For example, Meral Şimşek, who has two poems in this anthology, was sentenced to imprisonment by Turkish authorities for "making terrorist propaganda." This was in response to her work as a writer in general and also specifically pointed toward her short story "Arzela," which is included in the anthology *Kurdistan + 100: Stories from a Future State* (Comma Press), featuring twelve contemporary Kurdish writers imagining a country they could call their own by 2046. Also in this anthology is a nonfiction essay by Maha Hassan, who was banned from publishing in Syria due to her "morally condemnable" subject matter. There are many others in this collection who face similar obstacles. It is a mentally exhausting exercise to meditate on this contrast of power and oppression—and equally incredible to consider that these women continue to write from that deep well of courage and determination. I am honored that these writers have let me include their work in this book. To all the writers in these pages, I am grateful for your trust.

Exile and erasure are tools of the oppressor. This collection is the antithesis of erasure. In 2022, when the phrase "Women Life Freedom" rang out in protests transnationally and across digital spaces in response to the death of Jîna Mahsa Amini, many in the Kurdish community felt a twinge of pain and frustration at the lack of recognition for where this outcry originates. "Women Life Freedom" comes from the Kurdish "Jin-Jiyan-Azadî," which is a verbalization from Kurdish women's liberation movements. More than that, though, there was pain for the erasure of Jîna's name and identity as a Kurdish woman. Arrested by the Iranian state for improperly wearing her hijab, the protests in response that spread worldwide were not anti-hijab campaigns but more about the right to choose. The martyr who sparked the revolution that famous writers such as Marjane Satrapi have written about was a Kurdish woman. Why is it important to recognize her as Kurdish? Why is it important to note the origins of "Women Life Freedom" as Kurdish? Because of the way that Kurdish women are erased from the narrative and Kurdish cultural production is co-opted. More than that, it was the Iranian state that forced Jîna to go by her "official" government name, so it perpetuates further violence when she is not referred to by her Kurdish name in death. It perpetuates further violence when a phrase from Kurdish women's freedom movements is used in spaces where Kurdish culture and existence is suppressed and criminalized. To gain a deeper understanding of these contexts and implications, turn to "Why 'Jîna': Erasure of Kurdish Women and Their Politics from the Uprisings in Iran" by Farangis Ghaderi and Ozlem Goner. The goal here is not to defame the power and necessity of this movement for Iranian women (and Kurdish women alike). The point here is that within feminist solidarities, there must be a recognition of Kurdish women's roles and contributions in order for true liberation and justice to take place. This book uplifts and spotlights the role that Kurdish women (past and present) play in social, political, and cultural progress.

∴

To end on a note of homage, I turn to one of the pleasant memories my mother shared with me that has remained vivid in my imagination. In Baghdad, when the summer heat was strong and the home was without air conditioning, my mother and her siblings would sleep on the roof of their house—what she referred to as an "upper courtyard"—to feel the breeze. This was not unique to her family but a common practice in their neighborhood and region. The image of "an upper courtyard" always seemed so elegant to me as a child, especially in contrast to the other images of sparsity I held in my mind (like one small chicken split between twelve people for dinner). The image of my mother and her siblings sleeping outside in the courtyard in the summers felt important to me; feels important to me. There's something about them all calm, gentle, and soft under the stars. This book would not exist without my mother. The title, *Sleeping in the Courtyard*, is a nod to her and her siblings, who raised us within Kurdish traditions, within Kurdish pride, within Kurdish love.

Editor's Note: On Transliteration and Spelling Choices

Given that the Kurdish language in its various dialects is not so easily transferred directly into the Latin alphabet, you will find that one Kurdish word can have several different spellings in English, based on who is writing it out. For example, the term of endearment "gyan" ("my dear") is also often written "gian," interchanging the *i* and the *y*. Or at times it's even written out as "giyan" combining the best of both worlds. Another example is Sulaymaniah (also referred to as Slemani or Suly), the name of a culturally rich city in Southern Kurdistan that, when spoken, tends to sound more like the first *S* and *l* rub together and the *u* is rushed over (hence the alternative usage of "Slemani"). I've seen this city spelled at least five different ways, with each variation showing up regularly, not idiosyncratically. Just look at the bios of Kurdish figures and you'll see a wide range: Sulaymaniyah, Suleimani, Sulemani, Suleimani. We can also consider "thank you," which shows up as both "spas" and "supas," the *u* becoming just a *hint* like in the other example above. One of my own poems included in this collection was once published as "Kourban" but now as "Qurban," given that my family and other Kurds in my life tend to spell this intense term of endearment as either "Qurban" or "Quarban." It's important to note that there isn't really a "right" or "wrong" or "definitive" choice when writing a Kurdish word in the Latin alphabet. It's all an approximation, getting as close as one can to replicating the beauty of the Kurdish language in a language and alphabet that is not able to capture the fullness of each dialect. Finally, within this diversity in Kurdish spelling, rather than seeing varied spelling choices as a "lack" to be contained or "fixed," we can shift to see this as a reflection of the living, changing, pluralistic nature of language and dialect.

Additionally, for any works in the collection that were previously published or written using British English spelling, I have decided, in conversation with translators whose work is in this book, to keep the UK spelling. It feels important to not automatically homogenize to US English—especially with previously published work, as this would counteract the heart and power of this project, which is to bring together diverse voices from different parts of the world, which becomes even more evident in the different spelling preferences.

SLEEPING IN THE COURTYARD

HAJJAR BABAN

Broken Ghazal with Words

I prayed words
in my mind wouldn't change the ones I said when sobered, swords

of uncoupled verbs. *I know I'm doing better—*
I said it with so little words.

But sheltering my hate made it
happen more. Bubbles, shards, flakes. The words

left for my countries might never enter
me. I only learned yesterday how to track the image with words,

dried rose hips browning with dreaded weeds and a mask
on the ground. Even when I first said my name, wrongly, I worded

it beyond my first thoughts. هاجر whose first letter looks like a rose,
and some mistake meaning "stone." And my last, بابان which my father never told

me did not actually mean "two doors."

In Another Dream

for me, the whole world opens
I say sorry, sorry, excuse me
when I'm awake I'm asleep when
it's light in my room I pass
Slemani's waterfall, the sun agrees—
this word in Kurdish, so *foreign*:
after replacement

Where My Father Apologizes

in English, no utterance of a stutter
I wait by the phone He's asleep
he wades the ocean to get to me I know
the world, all the language terrors
no one will teach me
how to look at a face
to memory-wake.

ZHAWEN SHALI

لەدوێنێدا

من سێبەری ئەو ڕۆژانەم
هەتاو بیری چۆتەوە
بەپەنجەرەیانا تێپەڕێت

قۆڵم لە قۆڵی ئاسمان گیرکردووەو
لێوم لەگەمەی ئاگردا
خەون پڕە لە جێهێشتن،
شیعریش بینینەوەی لاشەی ئاشنایەکە
لەسەردێڕی دڵتەزێنی هەواڵێکدا،
بێبەریم لە زەوی
ماندوو لە جەنگ..

ئاو بوویت
ئەبوایە لێگەڕێم بڕۆیت
کەلەجێی خۆی هەڵکەنرێت
سەنگینە
بەرد.

ئاوێنەی شکاوی تۆم
تەماشای چی دەکەیت؟
خۆت لەهەزار پارچەی جیاوازدا

4

Yesterday

—Translated from the Kurdish (Sorani) by Arash Saleh and Holly Mason Badra

I am the shadow of those days—
the days the sun forgot
to radiate through the windows.

I linked arms with the sky
and touched my lips to the flames of the fire.
Dreams are replaced with leaving
and poetry is revisiting a familiar cadaver
in an oppressive headline of news.
I am deprived of land
and tired of war.

You were water—
I should have let you go.
The moment it is dislodged,
heavier becomes
the rock.

I am your broken mirror.
What are you looking at?
Yourself?
In a thousand different pieces?

گەر نەهاتنت نەبوایە
ئەو هەموو ساڵە چاوەڕوان نەدەمام
سەری خۆم بە پیاسەی ناکۆتای شەقامەکان
نەدەکێشا،

وڵاتانم بەدوتا تەی نەدەکردو
تەنانەت لەناو فڕۆکەیشدا بۆت
نەدەگریام.

گوتت دەگەڕێمەوە
زەنگەکانی کلێسا سێجار لێیاندا

موسوڵمانان بەدەوری مەککەدا تەوافیان بەست
لەمەیدان چوار سەد چرا بۆ پێشوازیت داگیرسان،

مناڵی لەبەردەم سیانزە کۆڵانی جیاوازدا چۆکلێتی راخست و
یوسف کە هەر قەرار بوو پارچەیەك لە کراسەکەی
بۆ ماڵی ئێمە بنێرێت
نەگەیشت و
ئەیوبیش لە کووخە چکۆڵانەکەی خۆیدا
گوێی بۆ گلەییەکانی ئەحمەد شەماڵ رادێرا..

If it wasn't for your absence
I wouldn't be waiting so many years.
I wouldn't bang my head in the endless spinning streets.

I wouldn't pass through countries to follow you.
I wouldn't cry on an airplane.

You said you will be back.
The church bells sounded three times.

Pilgrims circled Mecca.
In the square, four hundred lights were lit to welcome you.

Childhood becomes thirteen alleys
in front of each there stands a vendor of chocolates.
Joseph who was supposed to send us a piece of his coat
has not arrived.
And Jacob, in his small hut,
was listening to the complaints of Ahmad Shamal.

شەوێکی بێماڵ

مەسەلەکە راهاتن بەو دنیا نوێیەوە نییە
هەر خۆی راهاتن بە ژیانەوە
کارێکی ئاسان نییە،
من هەمیشە ئەوەم گوتووە

گەردوون گەمە سیحرئامێزەکەی خودایە و
ئێمەیش لە باشترین حاڵەتدا
پاڵەوانی سێرکین..

سیزیفێک تەرمی ئایندەی داوە بەکۆڵیا و
چاوەروانی پەرجوویەکە بۆئەوەی نەمر بێت..
بەڵام ژیان بزمارێکی تیژە لەژێر زمانی ئەو رۆژانەی
کە دەبێت بێدەنگ بیت

بۆیە هەندێکجار دەبێت وەک مناڵێکی عەجول
بەرد بگریتە ماڵی خودا و
دەست و پەنجەت لەگەڵ ئاگر نەرم بکەیت،

بە وێنەی میهرەبانیی دۆڵفینێک بۆ ژیان پێبکەنیت و
بەلاتەوە سەیر نەبێت
رووبار شمشێرێکی نێرینە بێت و
بە تاوانی شەرەفەوە
سەرت ببڕێت..

ژیان شەوێکی بێ ماڵەو
بەسەر پشتی کۆڵانەوە
من پشیلەیەکی ئاوارەم..

A Night with No Country

—Translated from the Kurdish (Sorani)
by Arash Saleh and Holly Mason Badra

To get used to this new world
is not the problem.
Getting used to life
is not that simple.
I have always said so.

If the cosmos is the magical fun of God,
then we are, in the best scenario,
heroes of a circus . . .

Sisyphus is carrying the corpse of the future
expecting a miracle to become eternal.
But life is a sharp nail under the tongue of those days—
the days that enforce silence.

This is why sometimes, just like a mischievous child,
you need to throw stones at God's windows
and wrestle with flames.

Just like a gracious dolphin, smile at life,
and do not be astonished
if the ocean is a sword
that sacrifices you
in the name of honor.

Life is a homeless night
carried on the back of an alley
and I am an adrift cat . . .

ئەی شەو

لەژێر پێی گەرمی سپێدەیەکا

بەچۆکا بێ، تا هەمووان ئەوە بزانن

سبەی رۆژێکی تر نییە

رۆژێکی تر مومکینە تەنێ چەمکێک بێت

لە فەرهەنگی فریوەوە دزەی کردبێتە نێو زوبانی گەردوونەوە و

من بێبەریم...

قەدەرم

لەبیرتە ئەو شەوانەی

وەک کۆڵەپشتێک

بەشانمەوە خۆت هەڵواسیبوو

خەرەندگەلی نامۆت پێ بریم و

لەنێو زیندانا

زیندانی ترت دروست دەکرد

مرۆڤگەلی هەمەچەشنت هێنایە وجودمەوە و

رێگا کۆڵانێک نەبوو

دەریچەی دەرچوونی هەبێ...

بەڵام من چۆڵەکەیەک بووم

بەرپێی هەورەکان کەوتبووم و

لە هەناوی ساردی ژوورۆچکەیەکی تەریکدا

دیوارەکانم بەدەنگی تۆ رەنگ کردبوو

تۆ لەکوێ بوی؟؟

ریسکی گرەوێک بووم

خوێنی بردنەوەم کردبووە کاسەی کاتژمێری ئەو رۆژانەوە

ونبوون میقاتی کردبوون

ماسییەک بووم

Listen night!
You need to kneel
in front of the warm steps of dawn
in order for everyone to recognize
tomorrow is not just another day.

"Another day" may be only a concept
absconded from the dictionary of deception
into the language of cosmos.
I am devoid of . . .
I am destiny.

Do you remember those nights?
Hanging in there,
you were just like a backpack on my shoulder?

Through strange ups and downs,
inside the jail,
there existed another jail
that introduced multiple shadows to my being.

The path was not an alley
with an opening for escape.
But I was a sparrow
being passed over by clouds
inside the interior of a cold and dark small room
painting the walls with your voice.
Where were you?

I had a huge risk to take.
I poured blood into the veins of time
without a prize in sight.

غروو ر و نازی نەورەسەکان
لەخشتەیان بردبووم،
ئەبوایە کلکی خۆم لە چنگ دڵەڕاوکێی ئەم زۆنگاوە
ڕاپسکێنم و
بڕۆم
بۆ ژیان ئەبوایە بەستەڵەکی ئەم ئەزموونە بپۆشم و
نەسووتێم
بەشوێن هەڵدانەوەی لاپەڕەی عومردا
بڕۆم و
بەسەر گۆنای ئاوارەی نیشتیمانەوە
ئەسرینی حەسرەت نەبم و
نەژاکێنم

ئەبوایە ڕێگا وێڵت بکا و
لەیەکەمین بینینەوە
وەک چاویلکە لەچاوت کەم،
ئەبوایە لە تیری قەدەدەرەوە دەرچم و
چوون سروودی نیشتیمانی
ئەفێنت لەبەر بکەم..

I was a fish
that was betrayed by the hubris and coquetry of the seagulls.
I had to cut off my tail
from the claws of that frantic swamp
and go.
I had to wear the ice of this experience
and not burn.

I had to follow pages of the age.
And go!
And fall!
off the displaced cheeks of motherland.
Not to be tears of regret
and not to wither.

AVA HOMA

Excerpts from *Daughters of Smoke and Fire*

Prologue

A woman alone on the mountain at dusk.

An invisible boot pressed against my throat, making my breath labored and helpless, and yet I couldn't go back and face my parents. Or my stifled future. Hidden behind a boulder, I hugged my knees and imagined my rage and pain whirling into a wildfire, burning down all the injustices.

Could my father have known what was going on? I wanted to tell him, to share this burden with him. My shoulders were already heavy beneath the daily cruelties of living as a woman in *La'nat Awa*, the damned place. This fatigue was incurable.

The sun had sauntered down, disappeared behind Lake Zrebar. A dozen shades of red burst open along the horizon.

Below, the narrow winding asphalt road was the hem around the hill's green skirt, embroidered with clusters of red and yellow wildflowers. The *shiler* flowers stood elegant and tall, flourishing across the rough Kurdistan plateau, defying borders. I yearned to be a *shiler*, but I was a garden of anguish, of loathing, of torment; my occupied homeland was a birthplace of death.

I stood up, my breath now coming in pants. I wasn't hiding anymore. "*Basa bas*," I shouted. "It's enough. Enough."

I started down the hill in a tumbling run and found myself unable to stop. Despite the chill of the evening, I started sweating. The wind whipped my headscarf, and I gained speed. I flapped as if I had wings.

As I ran, a wail escaped my chest. I was headed toward the main road, toward the world of men. The streets belonged to them. Judgmental men.

Hypocritical men. Their-honor-depended-on-women men. Cars hurtled around the curve, full of drunk drivers who honked as they spotted me sprinting down the hillside. They were going too fast for this road, too fast for their sluggish reflexes, and too fast for their old vehicles. A white late-model car careened down the winding road, kicking up dust. The wind roared in my ears. The white car and whoever was driving seemed to seek me out as a fellow traveler. I stumbled on a stone, crushing the shiny red poppies in the grass. And as I lurched, my untold stories tumbled inside me like pages ripped from a book and tossed, crumpled, into the wastepaper bin. An overpowering urge to scream my story, to expel it from beginning to end, seized me. Suddenly I could see the heads of all those Kurds crushed beneath tanks.

Descending the slope at a breakneck pace, my shouts crescendoing, I was unable to stop myself, this crazed woman.

A final lunge and I was airborne.

∴

A Hill of Multicolored Wings

My five-year-old mind could not identify the map drawn on my father's back and neck from the lashed scars of his time in prison. Wrapped in a beige towel at the waist and indifferent to the water droplets sliding down across the hacked frontiers on his bare back, my father packed some of the new baby's clothes and diapers and explained in a hoarse voice that he had to run back to the hospital.

Mama and my new baby brother, Chia, meaning "mountain," had not come home yet, and I was impatient to meet him. The events of that day were etched in some persistent cell in my memory. Baba got dressed, absently shoved my pants and doll inside a plastic bag, and gathered me into his arms. Wrapping my arms around Baba's neck, I saw tears in the corners of his eyes and the fresh drops of sweat on his receding hairline. It was stuffy in the house, the heater still blasting although it was well into March.

"Your head is crying," I giggled and ran my palms over his sharp stubble. "Angry skin. Porcupine." He carried me down the carpeted stairs that twisted in a perfect spiral from our hallway to the basement studio and knocked on Joanna's door.

Joanna opened the door, wearing her face-wide smile. "Congratulations, brakam!" She wasn't really my aunt, but she and my father called each other brother and sister. Joanna was dressed in a loose, green, ankle-length dress and a black vest, her hair tied up in a ponytail, her red lips the color of my father's bloodshot eyes. Her golden belt jingled as she walked, its many dangling coins clinking mellifluously together. I loved that she was always nicely dressed, how it set her apart from most women in Mariwan.

"Healthy baby boy. We'll be home tonight." Baba handed me to Joanna. "Could you please take care of Leila?"

Squeezed between them, I inhaled my father's signature smell of lavender soap, which mingled with Joanna's jasmine perfume.

"Of course. Hello, big sister!" she said as she tickled me under my arms. Baba thanked her and set down my bag next to the edge of the wooden door.

"Did you hear the news?"

"Hana . . . ?" Joanna asked.

"No . . . have you turned on the radio today?"

His own radio was always on, its staticky broadcasts a familiar soundtrack. Joanna's radio was usually on too, but hers played only mellow music, often Sayed Ali Asghar Kurdistani's soothing voice. She waved a hand in the air, swatting away the unheard news. "Believe me, I can live a day without tragedy, Alan! You can too. Newroz is coming. Your son is born. And we deserve a break, *brakam*, don't we?"

Baba's face twitched in a futile attempt to dispel the tears that pooled in the corners of his eyes. He turned his face away and crossed the tidy room to the dim main entrance of the walkout basement without another word.

"Let me get you a jacket, Alan," Joanna called out to Baba's hunched shoulders. The chill crept in even after he shut the door behind him, deaf to her words.

"I'm mostly made from water," I announced, repeating the little fact I had learned from Joanna the day before. She was the reason that, at age five, I could read. Her daughter, Shiler, could already spell too, and she was only twenty days older than me.

Joanna sat me in a chair next to Shiler, who was busy practicing the Kurdish alphabet her mother had taught her: *a* as in *azadi* (freedom), *h* as in *hemni* (peace), *n* as in *nishtman* (homeland)—everything the Kurds were deprived of. Born and raised in her mother's crowded prison ward, Shiler had learned to focus so intently on the task at hand that she completely disregarded the world around her, so she had only just now noticed my arrival.

When Joanna had been released from prison several months earlier, she and her daughter had moved into our basement while she looked for an inexpensive place to rent. My father had said they could stay in our house for free because he'd had a lot of respect for Joanna's deceased husband—his former cellmate, a leftist activist who had been executed. Since she had moved in, Joanna had painted the basement studio a light shade of green, and the grass no longer grew long and unkempt in the yard outside the large, spotless window.

Ava Homa

I was thrilled to have a new playmate, but Mama didn't like having Joanna and Shiler downstairs; she was suspicious of how Joanna had secured her release from prison despite being sentenced to death for stabbing a man. Baba had explained to me that in Iranian law, a man's life was worth twice as much as a woman's, so Joanna was to be killed in retaliation for taking her rapist's life. But the decision was eventually reversed.

"And God knows how!" Mama added.

Baba had stuttered when I asked what a rapist was.

"Go play with your dolls," he'd responded. I longed to know why the government punished everyone I liked.

Joanna now held a candy before me. "Mostly from water, ha? But what is the rest of your body made of: Chocolate?"

The orange-flavored candy was inside my cheek before I could answer. "No," I mumbled, mouth full.

"Honey?"

I shook my head.

"Why are you so sweet then?"

I laughed, holding onto the hem of my skirt. She kissed my cheeks. I wished Joanna had always been there, when Baba was too busy feeling bad for himself, Mama was too busy telling the world how wonderful she was, and Grandma was too busy praying for a grandson.

"Leila, have you had anything to eat?" Joanna asked with a hand on her hip.

"I found some yogurt. Ate it with sugar."

On her single burner, Joanna warmed up her leftover *shorabaw*, a traditional soup of beef and beans, though I found no meat in it.

"When will Mama and the baby come home? Do you think they miss me?"

"The baby doesn't even know you," said Shiler, looking up from her finished letters.

"Yes, he does! My brother would recognize me among a hundred girls," I declared. Joanna stirred some breadcrumbs into the *shorabaw*. I slurped the delicious soup and went on: "He'll recognize my voice, because I sang to him when he was in Mama's belly." Joanna confirmed that he certainly would.

"Joanna is sewing new dresses for you and me for Newroz." Shiler was the only child I knew who called her mother by her first name.

"You ruined the surprise, *avina min*," Joanna said.

Shiler took me to the sewing machine in the far corner of the studio, sitting by the cooler that acted as their fridge. On and around the hand-cranked machine, the fabric lay shapelessly, red printed with white flowers.

"Why don't you explain to Shiler how you celebrate Newroz here?" Joanna said as she washed the empty bowls in her tiny sink.

It was Shiler's first New Year's celebration outside of a prison cell, and I excitedly told her all about the gifts we'd receive—usually a crisp note and perhaps a toy—and how thousands would gather in the city center, where there would be lots of pastries, dancing, and bonfires. The celebrations would stop only when the Revolutionary Guards showed up.

"Why was my Baba crying?" I went to Joanna. "He likes Newroz."

She pressed my head against her chest. Her breasts were small, unlike Mama's. "You'll find out someday," Joanna said.

"When?" I asked.

"When you're an adult." She gently stroked the back of my neck and kissed my cheeks.

I pulled away and used the hem of my blouse to rub her saliva off my face. "I am an adult!"

Joanna laughed, a laughter that bubbled up from her core and erupted like a geyser. The wrinkles around her kind black eyes and her narrow mouth made her look older than Mama, though Baba had said she was younger. Mama had smooth skin, high cheekbones, and hazel eyes. No wonder people often assumed Shiler, with her straight black hair and beautiful eyes, was Mama's daughter and I was Joanna's.

"Tell me now," I insisted.

"Something terrible happened when your father was a child . . . I suppose it still makes him sad, especially now that he has children of his own." She straightened up, having said enough for one day. "I know—how about we pick some flowers to make a bouquet to welcome home Hana and baby Chia?"

Shiler and I whooped in eager agreement, and Joanna covered her hair with a white headscarf, grabbed her handbag, and led us outside. We combed the neighborhood for our bouquet, walking to the park to pick the first spring daffodils and poppies. When we picked the flowers, I felt their pain somewhere inside me; the hurt was very real. But I didn't say anything to Joanna and Shiler. When we had an armful of flowers, we stopped at a fruit stand, where a toothless man sold us strawberries so fat I could hardly hold them in my fist.

"Strawberries are my favorite fruit," Shiler said before stuffing her mouth.

"Well, you're very lucky, darling. Kurdistan has the best strawberries."

"Mine is pomegranate," I said.

"It must be in your blood, Leila. Your father is from the pomegranate capital, Halabja."

"I want to go there! I'd eat a hundred pomegranates."

"He is planning on taking you when the war is over. Hopefully soon."

I bit into a strawberry, its juices dripping down my chin, and asked Joanna, "What does your hometown have?"

"Olives. Kobani has delicious olives." Joanna wiped the corner of my mouth with a handkerchief.

The three of us watched as several butterflies, the first of spring, fluttered haphazardly against a sudden gust of wind, their wings glistening like dew.

"Oh, where were you all these years?" Joanna pressed a hand to her chest, shaking her head in amazement, water glittering in her joyful eyes. "What did eight years of bombing do to you? And to the bees and the dragonflies?"

"I'm a butterfly." Shiler sprouted imagined wings, her arms moving up and down in the air. "No, actually . . . I don't want to be a butterfly. I want to be an eagle."

"Though crows live a thousand years, I want to be an eagle." Shiler and I both recited the poem Joanna had taught us, in which a crow reveals to an eagle the secret to longevity: Settle for flying low and feeding on debris, and you'll live a hundred years. *"Chon beji sharta nakou chanda beji,"* the eagle refuses. How long you lived was irrelevant; what mattered was how you lived.

Joanna led us up the trail near the park, where we saw more and more butterflies. "Remember, girls, you can be anything you want to be. Don't allow anyone to make you believe otherwise. See, these beauties were simple worms once."

I thought I'd misheard that. "Worms? Worms can become butterflies?" I asked.

"Only caterpillars," Shiler corrected her mother. "Not every worm." Among the things I did not understand that day was how right Shiler was.

Neither of us knew if we were caterpillars or earthworms. Nor did we know if the tight, dark days of hanging upside down was the onset of death or a necessary part of an incredible transformation.

Chia and my parents did not come home that night, so I stayed in the basement. Joanna tucked me in and crawled under the bedsheets, covering her eyes with a headscarf. Shiler snuggled against her. I lay down too, but my mind whirred with thoughts—of Baba's tears and pomegranates, of whether my baby brother had a song in his heart.

"Can I play with the toys, Auntie?" I asked. Joanna was already softly snoring, so I slid from beneath the covers and played with the horses and elephants Joanna had arranged on a corner shelf. She'd made them in prison out of breadcrumbs, beans, and newspaper strips to educate and entertain Shiler. Soon I grew bored and looked around, and my eyes landed on the fat TV set sitting on a chair across from the bed.

When he wasn't watching the news, Baba sometimes let me sit and watch old films with him. Since I couldn't understand the words, I invented dialogue in my mind. I pressed the power button on Joanna's TV.

A nightmarish scene played in an endless loop: people with blistered faces lying on the ground, huddled bodies sheltering against walls. Birds, cows, sheep, cats, dogs—every animal had dropped dead, like they were flowers that had been plucked from the earth.

"—Saddam Hussein gassed Halabja this morning. Within a few minutes, five thousand Kurdish civilians died in an aerial bombardment of mustard gas and nerve agents."

People had fallen on the spot while trying in vain to run away from the chemical attack, trying to protect a loved one, now also dead: a baby, a child, a spouse. They had died with open eyes, open mouths. Flies had nested on their lips and burned cheeks. Their flesh had turned black. There had been no protection from the murky yellow clouds of nerve gas and deadly toxins, not for the civilians.

A tremor of fear sprang up inside my belly, making me shiver uncontrollably, but I was rooted to the spot, staring at the screen. A woman had choked to death while fixing a helicopter toy for a small boy. A girl had died grinning, as if cut off in the middle of a mischievous joke. Some seemed to have perished slowly. A woman was twisted like a rope, vomit and blood on her clothes, her face crumpled with anguish. Thousands and thousands of bodies. Others had collapsed on the outskirts of town, trying to cross the mountains, running to imagined safety.

"Everybody's dead!" I shook Joanna, my tears soaking her blanket. She startled awake, squinted at the television for a few seconds, jumped up to turn it off, and held me tight under the bedsheets. Shiler still slept soundly beside her.

"Are we going to die, Auntie?"

"Hush, my darling. You're safe. You are safe with me." Joanna patted my hair, dried my tears.

"Baba said TVs are liars."

"Yes, they are. Yes, they are." She gently rubbed my back, singing a lullaby: Ly-ly-ly ... Her velvety voice gradually soothed me to sleep.

That night I dreamed that the butterflies I had seen earlier arrived in Halabja, only to be gassed to death. Millions of them lay dead on top of each other, a hill of multicolored wings.

Ava Homa

TRACY FUAD

Object Exercise

First you must gather the objects.
Open the polish and polish each object
until every object is coated in polish,
a thin film that takes on the shape
of the object. Then dissect every
object with a circumstantial blade.
When the object is fully dissected,
remake it, but more in your image.
Then use concise scissors to prune
the object, removing what wilts
or yellows. Turn up the object
sound. Then, dissect again. Hold
each piece to check for resistance:
if it withers, it's an object.
If it shudders, it's a subject.

Jin-Jiyan-Azadî

With lyrics from Säada Bonaire

A man hangs scarves and bags on hooks to make a winter garden—

Or I suppose, a market

Past the white gleam of the new pediatrics on Nostrand a man says *baby can I*—

In a state of irritation, in a nation of emergency—

None of this, the source, but everything I see I claim and it claims me—

And I can't really think without etymology

The more I push the language through the automated translator, the more it
  strips away

You are free becomes *excuse me*, then *forgive me*

Two German women sing flat English over the saz that the DJ "discovered" in
  a Communist-Kurdish Community Center

The lyrics bubble up above the melody: *you have to face/the facts*

Into Kurdish, back again, *I am curious about myself* becomes *I'm proud*

Subject becomes *object*, and *object* becomes *everything*—

I follow the thread to a state that is not

∴

On the phone Carlos says Kurdistan is a blue ocean market

I say no, the sharks are feeding; the water is already red

And plus, I'm not interested in money

But he still tells me to snap up some property, in case it does become a
country—

The face in the mirror/Talks to me

The mirror in the mirror/My speech

∴

A girl says art is the last black market, that art is the quickest way to clean dirty
money

What I know about value is that it rises over time

Like the sea

I propose to no one that even irritation could feel good to someone dead

But then: that's not how the dead think

I'm born into the crush of the Uptown 4, held in place by the hot populace

We slide up Manhattan like public womb on a track

If prayer exists, I think, then this is it

In Union Square I shout *JIN – JIYAN – AZADÎ* into the bitter with the anarchists

A man asks *who is Afrin?*

And I recall that if you google *Afrin*, every image is of Afrin® Nasal Spray: *No
Drip* or *Severe*

City, I say, *and it's burning*

And on YouTube, it's *Newroz* and a man is playing saz on a chair amid the
rubble

Singing *Afrin, malomin—Afrin, my home*

∴

Of course the saz was just a backdrop for the DJ to play against, to overdub

For the club to taste, a carpet from faraway on which to wipe one's feet

A single note can start to overtake a song

Posing the question, how much can a single vessel hold?

The more I try to press my irritation into joy, the more the language dries and
turns another

Still I navigate to *KurdChat.com*, a room with no one in it

It isn't that I want to feel sublime at every moment

But I just don't feel things anymore the way I used to

JÎLA HUSEYNÎ

پرسیار

سەرپۆشە شڕەکەی دایکم
دەس بەرداری سەرم نابێ و
ئەڵێ: من هی داپیرەتم
رەنگە ئەویش لە داپیرەی خۆیەوە بۆی بەجێ مابێ
سەریشم پەنجەرەی تاقبازی بەرەو ئاسمانە
حەز ئەکا رۆژان میوانداری هەتاو بکات و
شەوانیش مانگ و ئەستێرە.
چاویلکەیەکی قەترانیش لەدایکم بۆ ماوەتەوە
ئەڵێ: دنیا هەرە ئەمەیە تۆ ئەیبینی
لە گەڵ هەر گرمەی هەورێکا، قارچکی سەد پرسیاری
دووپات و تازەش
لە چاوانما هەڵ ئەتۆقێت.

Question

—Translated from the Kurdish (Sorani) by Farangis Ghaderi and Rinat Harel

My mother's worn scarf

does not leave my head alone.

It says: "I am your grandmother's."

It might have been her grandmother's too.

And my head is an open window to the sky,

wishing to host the sun at day

and the moon and the stars at night.

My mother also left a pair of pitch-black glasses.

It says: "This is the world as you see it."

With every thunderclap, a mushroom of a hundred questions

old and new

sprout in my eyes.

که خەو بە تۆوە ئەبینم

خەو ئەبینم

دەستم ئەگری و لە تۆفانی سەرسامیدا

بەرەو کەنار ئەمرفێنی

بۆ بەیانی....

خۆت تۆفانی

لە خەوما تۆ

کورە باڵا بەرزەکەیت و

دەس هەڵئەبڕی

لە باخەکەی دراوسێتان

سێوێک ئەدزی و ئەیدەی بە من

دائەچڵەکێم

باخەوانێکی توورەیت و

سێوەکەت لێ دائەشارم.

هەرچی شەوە تۆ پاڵەوانی خەوەکان

تۆ ئەستێرە و شاخ و ئاسمان

جوانی و بزە و مێهرەبانی....

بۆ بەیانی؟

پێشکەشە بە کورتە شیعرەکانی خانمی نەجیبە ئەحمەد بە نێوی "وردە گڵەیی"

When I Dream About You

*—Translated from the Kurdish (Sorani) by Farangis Ghaderi
and Rinat Harel After Najiba Ahmad's "Usual Gripes"*

(1)

I dream that

you take my hand and in a storm of turmoil

rush me to the shore.

In the morning

you are the storm itself.

(2)

In my dream, you

are the handsome boy

who stole an apple from the neighbour's grove

for me.

I wake up.

You are an angry gardener and

I hide away the apple.

(3)

Each night, you are the hero of my dreams.

You are the star, the mountain, the sky.

You are beauty, smile, and kindness . . .

In the morning?!

MAHA HASSAN

Excerpt from *In Anne Frank's House*
—Translated from the Arabic by Addie Leak

Letters to Anne

Context: Maha, a Syrian Kurdish writer in exile, has been chosen as writer-in-residence in Anne Frank's family home in Amsterdam, where she is plagued by nightmares about the Holocaust. When she realizes that the house is haunted by Frank's spirit, she decides to face her fear by writing letters to Anne, just as Anne wrote to her imaginary friend Kitty in her diary. This is one of her first letters.

Tuesday, October 30, 2007

Dear Anne, it's about time we came to an agreement. Soon I'll have been in the house for a month, and I'm still walking on eggshells. I'm scared to bother you every time I come in, and I don't dare go into your room or upstairs. Maybe we need to put some rules in place—what do you think?

See, I'm talking to you out loud, describing everything I do so you don't feel weird around me. I describe the foods I cook and translate the names of the songs I listen to. I even tell you about every visitor before they come so you'll be part of my life and won't feel like an outsider.

You have the right to remain in this house. So do I.

We each have to recognize the other's right to be here.

This is your home, I'm aware. But now you're dead, and they offered me the chance to stay here, in this home you lived in sixty-five years ago. So we're here together; we'll share the place.

I could've gone back where I came from and left you the house, but you know someone else would take my place; I'm one of the few who believe you're still around.

You wouldn't gain anything from my absence. And as for me, the woman on the run, I'm always fleeing, turning page after page but leaving them blank, or unread, always convinced there'll be another page for me somewhere else. That's why I decided to stay. Staying means I've conquered my fear; it means I'm regaining some of my confidence in place; it means I'm independent.

Can't you see how important that is to me?

We're two very different women. I belong to a place, a time, and a culture that are completely different from yours. But we're more alike than we are different because we're both obsessed with writing.

You weren't a zealot when it came to religion, and maybe if you'd lived longer, you'd have been like me, setting religion aside. You're a writer; nothing mattered more to you than writing. I'm the same.

More unites us, Anna—as the Dutch call you—than separates us, even though I was born nearly thirty-seven years after you in a part of the world you may not have heard of, where I come from a people you know nothing about and speak a language you've never heard.

Here I sit, listening to Arabic and Kurdish music. And your spirit hovers about me.

I cook *molokhia* and *yaprak* in oil, two dishes you don't recognize. But I'll tell you about them and invite you to join me. We're living together, so let's spend time together. You don't know Arabic, so I'll translate my writing for you. We exist here together—culturally separate, but alike.

Your life's most consistent theme was flight. Mine's the same.

First you fled Germany, from the Nazis; then you fled from this beautiful home; then, because you're Jewish, they took you to a concentration camp.

I fled from a country I'm not even sure I can call mine—though I loved it in spite of the pain it caused—and soon I learned to be good at fleeing. I got used to it.

I know you understand me. You were a free spirit who quarreled with everyone. I'm the same. Everything I did was for the sake of my freedom.

Now here we are, the two of us together: me, born in 1966 in Aleppo and you, born in 1929 in Frankfurt. You, who speak German, Dutch, French, and maybe Hebrew, and I, who speak Arabic, Kurdish, and French, we're brought together in your home, in the Merwedeplein apartment, your family's refuge after fleeing the Nazis, now my refuge as I flee my fear. You understand me well because you're a writer, because you're a woman, and because you yearn for freedom.

We'll share the apartment, then. We can each enjoy our freedom without bothering the other.

The apartment is big, so we needn't argue.

I'm going to keep your parents' bedroom, and you'll keep your room. As for the living room, we can share it. I'll need it for writing.

I like to put my computer here, on the small desk by the big window looking out onto the big square, the light-filled square, green and busy: Merwedeplein.

I won't enter your room unless it's necessary. I won't touch anything in it. I'll leave everything as it is: the writing desk, the pictures, the armoire, the sofa . . .

But in return, I ask that you not use the bathroom or powder room; in any case, you won't need them, because you're dead. And your wandering spirit, in my opinion, will be just fine with the living room and bedroom.

Don't think for a second that I'm giving myself special treatment—it's just that the needs of the living outweigh the needs of the dead. And I'm alive, still alive, and I need more space than you. That's why I'm keeping the bathroom and powder room just for me.

As for the kitchen, no problem—use it whenever you want.

See, I'm being open with you, I'm not hiding anything; I respect your presence in this home, I even chat with you.

I'm a homebody, so I don't think you'll be too bored around me; I love to stay in, to write and read. When I get fed up with that, or when I'm feeling depressed, I sleep. And when I want a change, I cook or watch TV . . . In other words, I was made for a life lived at home, not outside, so I won't leave you alone for long. Every now and then I'll go out to shop or stroll or meet up with friends, but I'll always come back so that you're not alone at night. Eventually I'll go back to Paris—but while I'm here, I'll never leave you alone. I'll take the edge off your loneliness, like you take the edge off mine.

See, the doors are all open. I'm leaving the computer and papers out for you. I'm not hiding anything. The door to my room is always open, and you don't need to ask permission before entering. See, I even shower with the door open; I don't want you to feel out of place here. And I'm the same, Anna—as the Dutch call you—I don't want to feel out of place, either.

From now on, when I talk about the apartment, I'll stop saying, "Anne Frank's apartment." I won't say, "I'm staying in Anne Frank's home." Or "It's getting late, I'll head back to Anne Frank's house," or "Let's meet at the house, Anne Frank's house." Instead I'll say: "My apartment." I won't say, "I'm staying at a house, at number 37 Merwedeplein." Instead: "It's getting late, I'll head back home" or "Let's meet at the house, my house." I have to feel that this place belongs to me; I have to feel it's mine.

Maybe you're wondering, like I am, why I'm talking to you. Why I'm writing to you.

I can't give you a clear answer. But the feeling that we're here together in this place, at 37 Merwedeplein in Amsterdam, makes me feel like sharing my thoughts with you.

Maybe it's these moments, the moments I feel alone in the world. Alone, with absolutely no one. With no past or present, suspended in this mysterious home in Amsterdam, the temporary home that won't be mine in the end because, in the end, I have no place in the world. I've gotten used to moving and leaving places behind me. I've gotten used to not having my own place since I was uprooted from there, from the land I was born in, where staying didn't make me happy and I felt no sense of belonging. I became a seedling suspended in the breeze, or a feather tossed by the wind. I have no land to plant on or any place of my own. In these cruel moments of loneliness, I feel like you're the only being here with me. Maybe you didn't choose to be, but your spirit came back after your body died, to this very house that you left before you disappeared. Your last official, public presence was in this house. You left here to go to school, and to play and shop and visit friends, and it was here that you came home to every day. And it was here that you left on July 6, 1942, to hide in the annex.

Up to July 5, 1942, you were here openly. I can really feel you in this house, hear the sound of your breathing, feel you laughing uncontrollably. Every time I've looked at your photo, into those eyes sparkling with the hope and craftiness of a smart young woman, I've said to myself: Anne is definitely still here. There's no way that hopeful smile belongs to a dead person.

This home is the reality, plain as day in front of me. A real home.

Home is the foundation.

You've been dead for years, but the house still bears your name. Everyone points: The Frank family lived here, Anne Frank lived here. I'm the same; I tell people, *I'm living where Anne Frank lived*. This is still your house, then. Home is the self.

Do you know how obsessed I am with houses, I, who have never had a house?!

That's why I feel this way, spiritually displaced, like I don't have a house, or a family, or a homeland. I just roam from one place to another. That's what they call exile, dear. It's an exile I first tasted when I was still there, when I felt alienated from everyone around me and dreamed of migration; then I carried my life of alienation to another land, other people's country. A country that doesn't become ours no matter what we do, because we weren't born in it.

I've had rental contracts in my name in France, I have the legal right to reside there, and I've had a landline and a meter registering my electricity use, but, deep down, I've always felt like a guest there. The displaced person, the refugee, the exile—they're a perpetual guest in the world. It's difficult for them to own any place.

But writing helped me, transforming itself into a place I could inhabit and becoming home to me. I try to live inside it, to make it my mother and daughter, my family and homeland. And so I write.

In some ways, writing is what displaced me. You could say I'm contradicting myself; I've said before that writing saved me, that it gave me a new personality and a new fate, yes—but there's no harder choice. Writing's not a luxury or something you do just for fun. I fled with it to set it free, and it became my burden. And now I pay the price for my letters from one day to the next, turning the page on safety every day and losing the world to gain writing. Because the two can't be combined, the world and writing. Writing's the end of the world, the antithesis of the world—of it or the people in it.

Anne, it's bedtime now, stop wandering around the living room. Look, we each have our own room. I'll go to sleep, and you have to go to your room now, the room I rarely go inside because it's yours. The room of the dead, or the dead room, because I don't use it for anything. I just show it to a few visitors here and there: This is Anne Frank's room, which she shared with Margo.

I don't know, maybe I've been playing one of your childhood games with you; for me, you're still that young girl eager to play, and writing is one version of that delicious game where we create the world we want to see. A lot of girls talk to dolls, inventing names and places and events to make those dolls come alive, like real creatures, through their games. Have I told you how I used to play with my brother, how he would play the role of the lady next door, and we would divvy up the house? My little sister was our doll, and she would play the neighbor's daughter. My brother would become a woman, and my sister became a newborn baby girl. We would change the world by playing. All children love games, as if they, as a group, resent reality and want to invent a different one; they prefer different roles and events and people inside it. And all writers are children, they dream the same dream—to exchange this world for another.

Now we're playing together. Anne Frank, the Jewish girl, who knows nothing about Arabs and Kurds and Muslims and countries where women are oppressed and killed, and Maha, the woman who's running away from everything, is scared of everything around her, who hadn't even heard your name and who hadn't dreamed, even in waking, that she would one day come to Amsterdam. See, we're playing in our own way: you coming back from the dead (god, how can they think you died?) and me, still alive (god, where's the proof I'm not dreaming or just playing at being alive?!). Let's play together and have fun with this world. Maybe, with the game's help, we'll shake off our fear of loneliness, injustice, and constant judgment.

So let's do it—let's play! Let's write. Let's change the world with the game of writing.

NARIN ROSTAM

زۆرانبازی

هەر جارەی تەلەفزیۆنە ڕەشوسپییەکە
تەقەتەقی لێ هەڵدەستا و
یاری زۆرانبازی پێشان دەداین،
باوکم
خۆی لێ دەببووە پاڵەوان،
دەبوو قاپێک شووتیی قەڵەو بخوات.
دایە
سەری شووتییەکانی دەپەڕاند،
ئێسکەکانی شووتیی ورد ورد دەکرد:
زۆرانبازە دۆڕاوەکە بوو.
ئەمن
ناوبژیوانێکی بێ فیکە
بە شۆڕتی خەتخەتەوە دەسووڕامەوە.
کە کارەبا دەکوژایەوە،
دنیا ڕەنگاوڕەنگ دەبوو.
باوکم
قاپی شووتیی بەرز دەکردەوە
بە ڕاستی ببوو بە پاڵەوان.
زۆرانبازە دۆڕاوەکە
سەری لەناو کۆشی و
لە حەمام
پارچەی قاپە شکاوەکانی لە گۆشتی دەردەهێنا.
ئەمن
شەش فیکەی ناو چپسی یانەسیب بە ملمەوە و ناتوانم ئەم یارییە ڕابگرم.

Wrestling

—Translated from the Kurdish (Sorani) by Shene Mohammed

Any sound that came from
a wrestling match
on our black-and-white TV
would make father
think himself a champion,
so he needed a fat plate of watermelon slices.
Mother
beheaded the watermelon
and shred its bones,
the losing wrestler.
I
walked around in striped shorts,
a referee without a whistle.
Any time the power went out,
the world became colorful,
father
raised the plate in the air,
a real hero.
The losing wrestler
head on knees
in the bathroom
taking pieces of a broken plate out of her flesh.
I
have found six surprise whistles inside bags of chips.
I carry them around my neck and can't stop this game.

شەش پەنجە بە دەستێکەوە

کۆمەڵێک پەنجەی قرتاو لە زبڵخانەیەکدان.
درێژترین پەنجە هیی جەنگاوەرێکە،
شەڕێک قەوما و شەرەفی نیشتمان
هاتە گۆڕێ و ئێ..
با دەست بە وشەوە بگرین.
تایەی لۆری زبڵرێژەکە
قرچەی لە شتێک هەستاند:
پەنجەی مامۆستای بیرکاریمانە
گەنگەرین پەڕاندی..
تا ئەو وانەی پێ گوتین
پێنج کۆ پێنج نەبوو بە دە.
با فوو لە عەلاگەیەکی ڕەش دەکا
پەنجەی دکتۆری تێدایە
،دکتۆر ئالوودەی هیرۆیین بوو،
سەماعە بە ملییەوە..
بۆ دۆزینەوەی سەرە سیفۆن
هەناوی تەنەکە زبڵ نەما نەیپشکنێ
مووسێک پەنجەی ژەهراوی کرد.
ئەم کارتۆنە بێ دەرگایە
پەنجەی مێژوونووسی تێدایە
مێژوونووس
لەنێوان وشەکانی (سەرۆک) و (بەرمیل)
فاریزەی لەبیرچوو.
پەنجەی پێنجەم و شەشەم
خاوەنەکەیان لێبووکێکە،
قرتاندی..

Six Fingers in One Hand

—Translated from the Kurdish (Sorani) by Shene Mohammed

There are some fingers in the dumpster.

The longer one belongs to a solider,

a war broke out and the honor of the homeland

came into the picture and then . . .

Let's not waste words.

The tires of the trash truck

rolled over something cracking:

a finger that belongs to our math teacher

chopped off, the onset of gangrene.

All through the years this teacher gave lessons,

five plus five never made ten.

The wind blows on a black plastic bag.

Inside, there's a finger that belongs to

the heroin addicted doctor.

Stethoscope hanging from the neck.

To find a needle,

the doctor looked into the gut of every dumpster,

skipping none,

poisoning his finger on a razor blade.

Inside this doorless cardboard

there's the finger that belongs to a historian,

the historian

who forgot a comma between the words

"president" and "oil."

The fifth and sixth fingers

belong to a puppet.

که دەگری و پەنجەکانی دەموچاوی دەشارنەوە،
دەیەوێ لە کونێکی گەورەترەوە
پێکەنینی جەماوەر ببینێ.

He chopped them off
just to see the laughing audience
through a bigger crack
when the fingers hide his crying face.

GIAN SARDAR

Excerpts from *Take What You Can Carry*

Dreams

This past January, a couple of months after they'd started dating, Delan disappeared from bed in a time that seemed more night than morning. When Olivia wandered downstairs, he'd already eaten breakfast, showered, and was sitting at the kitchen table with a newspaper before him. His hair was damp and clumped with curls, and the light through the window was strangely intense, one of those bright Los Angeles winter mornings with no clouds but a cold, devious bite in the air. Deceiving, like a candy lure from a stranger. On the radio, the newscaster's voice rose with excitement over a freeze warning, and Olivia pictured silvery orange groves and farmers glaring at the sky.

A kiss on his cheek. Then eggs cracked on the edge of a bowl, whisked practically to a froth. As the flame beneath the pan spread, she asked why he'd gotten up so early.

At first he said nothing, just watched the window with the paper in his hand while the radio announced that the Hillside Strangler had been arrested in Washington and a blizzard was pounding Chicago. As she poured the eggs, she realized he might not have heard her question, so she switched the radio off till he looked at her—or, rather, not so much at *her* as to the absence of sound. There was a vacancy in his eyes, a distraction. "You got up early," she said again, tracing the spatula in the pan in a figure eight. "How come?"

"Dreams."

"Of what?"

"Home." Still he held the paper in his hand and went back to watching the day. "Your eggs are burning."

By this point, she was used to sparse words when it came to what upset him, but still she tried. "Do you want to tell me about them?" she asked, though it was clear he did not.

He shrugged—not to indicate he might talk about the dreams but to categorize them as not worth the effort of explanation. "I just didn't want to be asleep anymore."

She shut off the stove and accepted his response without pushing, then watched him as she made her lunch, waiting to see if he'd offer more. Recently she'd inquired about transferring to the photo department, just as a secretary, an idea that made her boss roll up one sleeve of his shirt as if preparing for a mildly restrained fight. *Let's keep our eyes on our own desk, shall we?* Disillusionment had begun to thicken her days, filling and spreading into each minute. Though making a lunch might mean she'd be late, she didn't care—or so she told herself while her eye was on the clock.

"The Kurds. Fighting," Delan finally said, motioning to the newspaper in his hands. "That's what's happening. Always."

She sliced an apple. Apples reminded her of her childhood, and with each cut, she smelled their crush in driveways, that lazy bite of fermentation in the air. "You're worried about your friend?"

"This," he said, tapping the article with his index finger, *one two, one two,* "is about Iran. The Kurds in Iran. An uprising coming. Aras, though, him I always worry about. But it's a given he'll die."

She looked up sharply, and he smiled sadly.

"Everyone will. He, sooner rather than later. He's a Peshmerga; it goes with the territory. His life might be short, but he will make a difference. *Kem bizhi kell bizhj*: Live short, live proud."

"Live big and bold and brave. That's what my dad says. Similar. About impact. Making the most of your blip in time."

He let go of the paper. With his hand, he went to push back the hair on his forehead but stopped midmotion, pausing as if stunned in the glare of morning. For a while, he said nothing. Then he took a long, deep breath. "And yet here I am." Hand lowered, he traced his finger on the black of the headline.

"Delan. You do things. The protest at the federal building. The letters to Carter. Hundreds of people know who the Kurds are just because of you."

"Let's grill tonight. Make some calls, see who can come over. This weather is too good."

She looked to the window. "It's freezing outside. Literally. They just said that."

"It's not. It's fine. And I'm the one at the grill."

She loved the parties and he knew this and it was true, he would be the one at the grill. And she needed something to look forward to, to get her through the day—as did he, it was clear. So she finished making her lunch, set it next to her camera on the counter, and decided to pick up ground beef that was cheap and could feed a crowd. When she looked back at him, he was lost in the paper once more, side lit by the kitchen window on that biting January day, and she saw there were tears on his face. It took her a moment to spot them. So often had she seen him angry when he talked about home that to see this was as confusing as their Los Angeles day of sun and blue skies and air that stung with cold.

Right at the end of the counter was her camera. *Always get the shot*, he'd once told her. *Art makes a difference. And if someone's story, their pain or sadness, if that can impact someone else, it's worth the invasion.* She watched him now, knowing that if he could see what she saw, he'd want this as well.

Choices in terms of where to stand were limited without breaking the moment. So she went back to the counter, knelt on the linoleum, and without him noticing, lined up her shot with the window to his right. She inched over to exclude a stain on the wall but then moved back, liking the way it looked in the frame, then made sure there was more space before him than behind. The curtain on the other wall was drawn closed but thin, and light fell in diffused chunks, broken by the windowpanes. She waited till he looked up from the paper that was still in his hands, and when he did, his face shone just enough to catch those silent, gleaming tears, and she pressed the button. He must have heard, but he never acknowledged it. Just sat back and let the paper fall onto the table.

That night they had the party, and she had to stand outside with a blanket on her shoulders and grill because he was asleep. She'd known he would be the second she came home and found him grinning loosely in his chair. So she stood in the biting air and was mad. Mad that he'd arrange for this whole thing and invite all these people over and then check out and leave her in the cold. Mad that everyone had shown up hungry. Mad that he had so much to cry about, and she couldn't help with any of it. And when at last she went to wake him up, the spatula still in her hand and the blanket around her shoulders, she found him on the couch, his fingers skimming the rug. His breathing was steady even while the Eagles sang about a hotel in California and the people in the room caught the beginning and sang along loudly, relishing in location and fame and their luck to live in such a lovely place. His chest rose and fell. Without waking him, she reached down and lifted his hand so it was by his side, so no one would step on his fingers. Then she let him sleep, gone from wherever he'd wished to leave.

∴

The Distance of Separation

Night, morning, afternoon. The rusted, inching turn of the world. Somehow it feels as though life is flaunting its continuation. Sun bright. Clouds triumphant. The world is gorgeous and unruffled and unnoticing. This is what she's trying to reconcile: blinks of destruction amid beauty. Everything combined with the unfazed tick of the clock.

The picnic is still happening. Up in the mountains, but not where the fighting is. When Delan tells her this, his distinction falls short of comforting.

"Just key places is where they fight," he adds, seeing her doubt. "High up. We don't go there."

So she finds mountain-appropriate clothes—tennis shoes, long pants, a light-weight shirt. And she feels guilty to do just this, to keep going and be the one to wake up when others do not. To wash her hair and decide what to wear and think of photographs and love and fears and a future. In the mirror, she spots her necklace. The tree of life. A reminder of an eternal connection between this realm and that, the tree's branches touching the heavens. *Every time you raise your arm*, her father told her when he gave her the necklace, *I see your mother reaching for your hand.*

"It's a choice," Delan says when he finds her in his room, watching the street. "You're thinking about what happened. But it's a choice not to. You put it out of your mind."

She turns to him. Thrown. His tone borders on demanding. Impatient. Body angled as if he's ready to leave the room, as if he were ready to go from the moment he entered. "How," she manages to ask, "is that even an option?"

"You, who wants to control everything, your thoughts too—you ask how?"

"Not this. This is different."

"If you were to surrender after something like this, you would never live your life."

Flippant almost. As if he's just told her to deal with the fact that it's hot outside. "Here," she says, trying to keep her voice level, "that might be true. Because this happens. Things like this happen. But I can't just *do* that."

"Anywhere, this happens," he says. "Where we live, you see a man fall on the sidewalk from a heart attack or someone who's overdosed in a hallway—do you let it destroy you?"

"I let it *affect* me. Yes. And those are different than a *bomb*."

"Death is death. The same outcome. You who saw your mother—"

"Stop," she says. Anger splayed. Every inch of her pulses with it. She tries to breathe in, to clear a space within her for logic and rationale, but all she sees is this man she thought she knew, accusing her of being too soft. A man who's suddenly callous in the light of tragedy. "My mother," she says. "That did destroy me."

"But *this* was not your mother. That's what I'm saying. These were people you didn't know. You don't fold after this."

"I'm not allowed to feel for people I don't know? How *dare* you come after me for this."

"Come after you? I'm trying to help!"

"By telling me to move on? To get over it? How can *you* just move on? How can you be so unfeeling that you just move on?"

"I never said move on. You move *with*. You move with, but you move. That's the point. You cannot stop. But to do that, you need to put it out of your mind so you can. So you become a politician and fix things or be an artist and put it in your art. If you crawl into a cave and let this defeat you, *everyone loses.*"

For a moment, he just watches her, as if making sure his point landed. And this irritates her even more. As he opens the window to scan the street, she feels her words honing, pressing to a point.

"Is that what you do?" she asks quietly. "Put it in your art to help?" Her words are like a jolt. His back tenses, body gone rigid. "That's why you feel bad," she continues. "You think you don't do enough."

Now he turns to her. Shocked and irate. "Don't tell me I'm living my life wrong."

"There's no standard for what you have to do to feel okay. But *you* know. You know what you have to do, and maybe you're right and you don't do enough. The only thing I know is you've spouted a whole bunch of made-up rules that allow you to look the other way—all so you don't have to feel."

His eyes seem to actually fill with what he's about to say. And she feels it, an undertow of anger. The start of whatever he's about to say that will pull them in and strand them. From his words, there will be no getting back.

"*You,*" he finally says, "don't come from a world where you get to judge how *I* handle this."

A slam that renders her speechless. But one she's been waiting for, that she practically asked for. Words strip in her mind: *There it is.* All this time, it's been there, off in the corner, waiting. Now in the open. Thickening, filling into the silence. Her youth. Her vastly different childhood. The weight of his past, compared to the relative ease of hers. It's all right there. And the problem is that he's right. In some way, she's always known this. But what does it mean? That, she realizes, is the question. The crux of what she's needed to learn.

"You're right," she says.

There's surprise on his face, as if he's just glimpsed a swerve in the road.

"What you've been through," she continues, "*nothing* I've known will ever compare. But does that mean I don't have a point? That I can never tell you I wish you'd do something differently, because I didn't grow up the way you did? How does that work for our relationship if I get dismissed for my past? If nothing I say is valid?"

The questions hang. They're everything, these questions. She's never conjured them this clearly before, never assigned them these words, but they've always been there. A simmer beneath recognized worries.

"Of course not," he finally says. Outside, a horn sounds. "If that were the case, no couple would work unless they grew up in the same house."

A pause, and he leans away from her, searching the street through the window. Maybe he's just saying what he knows he needs to. He's still angry, that she can tell. And so is she. Despite his response, the questions remain unanswered.

"But you can't presume to know," he finally says. "You cannot tell me *me*."

"Then likewise. That works both ways."

From the street, a car honks again. And then another. For a beat, they are silent, held back as if tied to their own points of view, until again a horn sounds, and he leans out the window, calling to a man in an off-white pickup truck. Behind it, a caravan of cars stretches the length of the road.

"Maybe we just do things differently," she says.

"Clearly."

There will be no resolution. Not now. She watches him yell to the man again in Kurdish, watches his profile, and feels, starkly, sadly, the borders of themselves in a way she never has. All the memories tied to what passes before them, the layers of fears and hopes and regrets, the events that have made him see the world as he does and pass off what's happened as not that bad—all of it kept separate by the simple lines of his skin. She cannot know him. Not truly. *You cannot tell me* me. And though she knows that's the case for everyone, for no one can exist within another's mind or skin, it's how far apart they are in their history, their beliefs, that ultimately matters. After all, it's the distance of separation that creates the impact.

An assortment of cars and trucks curves around the base of the mountain, each one with multiple men crammed in the front seats and women in the back. Though Delan was offered the front seat, he wisely chose to sit next to Olivia, and in this, their battle at least hasn't escalated. On her other side, an older woman in a traditional dress that's a brilliant, iridescent beetle-green stares only at her folded hands in her lap.

The road is unpaved and rocky, at times more an idea of a road than an actual road, and after twenty minutes of views heavy with green and the shock of pink plum blossoms, they swoop upward on a road so narrow that the side mirrors brush shrubs and catch on branches. Now and then there is a blind curve, a switchback, and the sheer cliffs and the absence of land pull with a vacuum's energy.

You put it out of your mind. She closes her eyes, chin against her chest.

That family, they left.

You *don't come from a world where you get to judge how* I *handle this.*

They've barely spoken since they left the house, and now she's thinking of all the ways he lives in denial—even at home, in mundane ways, such as with a phone bill shoved into a drawer—*don't look*—or a bottle of gin that eases him toward sleep. Only now does she see how deep this goes, how dark the source. She feels sick. His life, his world might not be one she can be part of. All the lines she fed herself about differing pasts and backgrounds not mattering were just that—lines. Hopeful lies from the mind of a romantic, from someone who thought differences would fall in the way of true love.

That loose flutter of sadness. Never have they done this. Arguments over inviting another couple over for dinner, sure, or if it was time to fold and call a plumber, of course. But nothing that spoke to the core of them. To the core of *if* they work.

Green branches whip along one side of the car. Nothing is over, she tells herself, though it feels that something has indeed ended. Maybe just the glow of a new relationship. At best, that's it. She tries to not think, to just take in the world around her. Flares of dark red in the grass. Poppies. Growing in clumps, cupping the sunlight. Then a wide stretch of aspens, an ancient orchard. Bees rise from short white wildflowers in the grass. These rocks, she tells herself, long-gone shepherds once sat on these rocks. Again there is that pull, that connection, an anchoring to the earth, to the simple essence of their lives. And sadness. Because with the end of each distracting thought, she is right back to this: never has she felt this far apart from him.

Gian Sardar

HIVA PANAHI

Secrets of the Snow

My secrets are snow
Behind the big windows
The moment it falls the voyage begins
Everything muted and white
Voyage to fathom the cries
Voyage to God who kept abandoning us

Once I wore my red boots
I brought a candle to the grave of God
On my return my grandmother kissed me on the forehead
I knew it was time for a red fairy tale
To traverse the dark chambers
To reach the truth
The tales would come to our house
I saw the heroes sleeping
If only I could give them my multicolored pillow
The night of the heavy snow
My room filled with butterflies and water lilies
Till morning I sat with them in gardens
Snow all day
Snow all night

The next day the words of the sparrows were snow
The hearts of the doves became snow
I didn't find them to feed them

The neighborhood children were snow fighting
Snow covered the doors of the houses
The children's hands froze and were covered

The neighbor says the snow of the mountain is warm
It heals her pains
The snow was the hyacinth's secret
People left for the mountain
For the women of the town the Shadas[1] were forbidden
They gave them to trees
The trees made shade for the Peshmergas[2]
The snow was a mother, it knew about everyone
It carried unbearable pain
It fell from everyone's eyes
Everywhere filled with snow
How did the snow manage to remain in love
With so many of its white songs?

The snow came and left
The people of the city lived in pain
The streets didn't want the women anymore
In one night the people grew old
The snow was not enough
To cover the blood of the women
The blood of the virgins
The city did not know what to do with their corpses[3]

---

1. A traditional Kurdish shawl for young women, worn when they go to visit their loved ones.
2. Kurdish warriors.
3. The city referred to is Sanandaj, which is still sometimes called "Bloodshed City," after the great genocide of the Kurds in Iran from 1980 to 1985.

Even the stones and the earth were driven to leave
The voyage of the angels
The voyage of the snow
The stories of my grandfather were snow

It falls ceaselessly
White, white
Life instead of genocide
The snow is a big soul
The snow is generous
Everything has become white
The snow has a soft heart
It covers the bloodstained city

A Poet Was Murdered

The distances grow longer
everywhere The eyes scatter
everywhere
The sounds searched for you
everywhere Your eyes were found in
the streets Covered with snow

BAYAN NASIH

The Explorer Who Watched from a School Window

The Village of Hasar

I was born somewhere in the world. To the eyes of a child like me, Hasar was the best and most beautiful place in the world, obviously as long as I did not cross the border of our city. The village was a big enough place for me. Its valleys and surrounding peaks and hills, its big graveyard, its strange wheat, its red calves, its train tracks, the villages of Qumsal, Qarachikol, little flowing springs, crazy Omar, the fat little ones, hillocks, the Guldarawa pond and many others were all beautiful to me. Surrounding the village was a large, unknown world. My family's only wealth was the food they had to survive on from one season to the next. Our greatest wealth was one or two cows and their calves. Each of them had their own names: Yellow Cow and Red Cow. The cows brought much joy to our family. When they produced decent amounts of milk, our breakfasts were happier and richer. When one of our cows was pregnant, it was as if it were Eid. My parents spoke with so much joy and pride about the new calf. With this newborn calf, we enjoyed the yellow whey for three whole days, which was produced from the mother's new full milk.

One of the best things for children like us who grew up during the sanctions was the partying that took place in the village during summertime. Our curfews were shorter those nights, so we stayed out to play with our friends longer. One of my favourite things to do was to tie the ends of the women's sleeves together when they were doing the Kurdish dance in a line, so that when they wanted to move away from each other, they ended up pulling each other because they did not know their sleeves were tied together. Although they started laughing, the rest of us who played this childish trick were berated.

One of our other games was hide and seek. We turned those streets of the sanctioned land into our playgrounds, and we ran as best as we could to find each other. When I was six or seven years old, I had no proper toys. My toys were made of stones, wood, pieces of colourful glass, colourful fabrics. We fashioned plates, spoons and cups out of mud.

The Shoes of the Pink Doll

I had a strange habit in those days. I was always searching for new things, especially in trash cans! Sometimes I found colourful glass. One day, I found a very small pink shoe. I understood that it belonged to a doll. I liked the shoe so much that I dreamt of finding the doll for it. But this did not happen, and I asked my father (whom we called Kaka[1]) to find me a doll that could wear these shoes when he traveled to Kirkuk. My father was always kind to us. If he could not afford to buy us something, he would say, 'When I go to the city, I will ask around.'

Whenever my father travelled, I would spend all day waiting for him in the shade near the wall of our house or around the pool or at the mosque. Until then, I had not seen the city myself. As soon as my father alighted from the car, I ran to him. As always, he kissed my head. My first question was, 'Kaka, did you buy the doll for me?' My father always gave me a different answer, always in a calm tone: 'The store of the old man who sells dolls was not open today'; 'The Haji was sick and could not open his store'; 'Uncle Haji's wife was sick, he could not come to the store'; 'Uncle Haji went to Baghdad to go buy stuff for his store'; 'Uncle Haji's dolls were sold out'; or 'Uncle Haji's hands are rusty now, he cannot make dolls anymore.'

I would forget about the doll and start thinking about Uncle Haji, feeling bad for him. Even now, whenever I see Barbie dolls with extremely small shoes, my mind takes me back to when I only had one tiny shoe.

I Was Pippi's Explorer

When Astrid Lindgren wrote *Pippi Longstocking*, she brought the children of the world together. Pippi gave a new name to those children who look for things: explorers. I was an explorer.

One day, I returned home with my sister after we visited our cows. When I was a child I could not shepherd the cows alone, even near the village, which is why my sister Amina and her friends came along. They were put in charge, and each one brought along their younger sister to give them a hand when needed—for example, in leading the cows up or down a slope, or finding decent pasture

---

1. A Kurdish term used for older men, and is also used for older brothers as a form of respect.

and water. Later I was put in charge of taking the cows for a walk, and I took a younger sister as my own assistant. In the evening, we used to pass by an all-boys' school. Behind the school was an area where trash from the school was thrown. I had never seen it before.

Shepherding the cows introduced me to the school, which was on the other side of the village. One day, I found something new. It was a small pencil the size of my pinkie, and both sides of it had been sharpened. This made me so happy. I eagerly looked for more things in the trash. My search was not useless; I also found an eraser. As soon as I found the pencil and eraser, I became curious about school. What was a school, and what was done there? How was it? I had seen older kids with books walking around. They were called *students* and they were *studying*. School became my hobby.

Some days, I did not take the cows out. I simply left the house to go and look for things, to explore. Walking around the boys' school was my new favourite activity, and it was not long before I discovered that there was also an all-girls' school nearby. It was a two-room house made of plaster and concrete. They also had trash, but I did not find anything in their trash. I heard sounds coming from the school. This made me excited; what were they doing inside? The walls of the school were high, or maybe I was just short then. At home, I mentioned the school a few times and how I wanted to go there, but there was no answer as to whether they would allow me to.

One morning around the time school started, I was looking at the girls from a distance. They were dressed in blue with white bows in their hair. They did not look like girls from our village. I saw them all dressed up and neat while I was barefoot, wearing plain, drab clothes, my hair uncombed, and chapped skin on my hands. I felt very different from them, especially when the girls left the schoolyard and went to the classrooms. I followed them and hung onto the edge of a high window and kept looking at them.

The window had not only glass but also window bars, which is why no one could see me. But I saw them well. There were two rows of desks and two girls sat at each one. There was a teacher standing in the middle of the room. I pulled my head towards the classroom as best as I could to see what was happening.

After a couple of days one of the students, who was also my mother's relative, came and asked me if I was going to school. I replied that I wasn't. Another day, I was walking a few meters away from the school. When the noise from the schoolyard stopped, I slowly began walking toward the window. But the girl I spoke with seemed to know my secret, so she pointed at me from the class, and the teacher turned to me. This scared me, and my heart began beating fast. I jumped so quickly from the window that the plaster and stones scratched my hands and arms.

I Convinced Myself

I did not show my hands and arms to anyone, and no one at home asked me anything. The following day I took extra caution, but I still hung onto the window. This time, I was more prepared to run if anyone saw me. This was when the teacher opened the school gate, which was very close to the window. I was shocked and slowly climbed down. The first thing she said to me was a question: 'Do you want to come to school?' I replied 'Yeah!' with much enthusiasm. She told me, 'So come inside.'

The teacher, whose name I later learned was Teacher Fawziya or Miss Fawziya, took me inside and for the first time, I sat on a school chair.

'What is your name?'

'Bayan Haji Nasih.'

She softly said, 'Only say Nasih, you do not need to add Haji. Instead of saying yeah, say yes, okay?'

'Yes, okay.'

'How old are you?'

'I don't know!'

'What is your grandfather's name?'

'Kakaways.'

'Kakaways is your father's father, or your mother's father?'

'My mother's.'

'What is your father's name? Your grandfather?'

'I don't know.'

'Okay, go home and tell your family that you have registered yourself at school. Starting tomorrow, you will come to school. You will wash your hands and you will come wearing shoes. You will ask your parents to buy a school uniform for you. You can wear black or blue and white bows. If you have an identification card, you can bring it with you; if not, your parents have to make one for you. And don't forget to ask what your grandfather's name is.'

I was in shock with joy and fear at the new way I was addressed. Someone from the city was speaking to me! I stuck myself like asphalt to the chair until the teacher got up and asked me to go with her. She said, 'Say hi to your parents and tell them tomorrow you are coming to school.'

When I left, I felt like a bird. Instead of walking, I was flying. I did not stop until I reached home. When I got home, I created a fuss and did not know how to talk about the way I had been registered at school, except for jumping up and down and repeating, 'I registered myself! I registered myself at school.'

A Big Colourless Dress

By early evening, my family all understood that I was going to school, and the teacher had already decided that I was. My family broke down into two groups. Some of them thought I was going to learn to be a whore. I did not know what that meant. One of my sisters said, 'Go so that we are no longer ignorant.' My father quietly agreed. He said, 'My daughter is going to be a scholar.'

For me, nothing existed other than school the next morning. What was I going to wear? One of my sisters had a pair of sandals. That was one solution, although they were bigger than my size. What about a dress? I had a big dress that my father had tailored for me, but there was no colour left in it. I wore that one. I woke up early that morning. I did not need to change because I had been ready since the evening before. Only the chapped skin on my hand had not healed. I stood in front of the school gate very early that morning. I did not know what to do or how to act. When I went in, everyone knew it was my first day, and they showed me the first-grade classroom.

The two teachers who were from Kirkuk arrived in the same car as the teachers who were at the boys' school. Miss Fawziya invited me to the teachers' room. She gave me a book, two notebooks, a packet of pencils, a sharpener and an eraser. I wanted to fly with joy. The teacher showed me how to put a cover around the book and said I needed a backpack. She reminded me to buy a school uniform and to bring my identification card to school. The girls' school consisted of only two classrooms. The class I was looking at from the window was that of the second grade, and there was another that had recently been built from mud. The house was only two rooms and a patio, which was made of stone and plaster. The teachers' room and the second-grade classroom were white with concrete floors, but the first-grade classroom was all mud. There was a blackboard and a window. There was a total of ten or twelve students. Some of the girls travelled from Goldara to school. The classroom had six pairs of desks and chairs. There were three on each side. I sat next to a girl in the third row whose home was close to mine. One of the girls from Goldara fought with me, and this was a new experience. I did what I could and said, 'I will tell my sister Marjana. Everyone is afraid of her. She is very brave.' I don't know to what extent this was true, but that is what I thought.

A Cloth Bag

In the early days of school, my sister Jamila made a cloth bag for me. My biggest concern the first couple of days was my shoes and my clothes. Some of the children wore black plastic shoes, which had space for air. The daughter of one of the teachers wore a dress that came down to her knees that I found so beautiful. I told my father every day, 'Kaka please, buy me a dress like the one of the teacher's daughter— the one that has black and white dots on it.' Each time, though, my father replied, 'I could not find it.'

I wanted a dress and a pair of shoes for school so badly that I cried. I finally got a pair of plastic shoes, but there was no news of the dress. One afternoon, my father returned from the city and said, 'I got you black fabric for your school dress.' Out of joy, I gave up on the dress of our teacher's daughter. I was just happy to have a dress at all because Teacher Fawziya asked about it every day.

My oldest sister made a dress for me and sewed two large pockets in the front. On the pockets, instead of white collars she sewed old white fabric on it. When I put it on, it was very big and wide. I started crying. My sister said, 'Bring it to me, I will fix it for you.' She washed the dress and hung it to dry. In the morning, luckily for me, it had become smaller and when I wore it, it came to my knees. That morning, I went to school with pride.

Most days, the school gate was closed when I was there. That day, I saw one of the girls from Goldara on my way to school. When she saw my dress, she said, 'The white on it is dull and the pockets look ugly.' The comment hurt my feelings, but it still did not steal my joy entirely because for me, the fabric was white enough. My desire for school meant that I worked hard, and I became a top student just in my first month. In the second year, the administration decided to put both the girls and boys into one building. This put pressure on some of the girls, and they quit school.

When I finished sixth grade, my family allowed me to go to Kirkuk for secondary school. I reached high school, and in order not to give up on school I had to move to the city. I lived in the Rahim Awa neighbourhood with one of my uncles and his family.

It was during this time that the oppressive Baath regime forced people to leave their homes and turned the village into dust. Our memories were all destroyed; the noise children made at Hasara school, the children's games, the shepherds' songs, the sweet old women, the beating of hearts, our parents' memories, my grandparents, the animals and birds—everything disappeared.

What remains most important are my own memories and the years I lived there. They never get old. I will never forget the window I climbed; it will never collapse. That window opened onto a new world for me and gave me a chance in life.

I don't know what happened to Teacher Fawziya, but I want to thank her in this writing. Instead of scaring a child like me, she respected me. She changed my life by registering me at school. She gave me wings to fly, and I used them well.

LEILA LOIS

Last Light

There is a coherence in things.
　　　　—VIRGINIA WOOLF

I've made a tradition of chasing sunsets
all the distal way to the lighthouse,
through the blushing last breath of day,
to watch as the tall ecru tower,
ignites a shawl of light
through violet dusk.

I see the candles my mother placed
in our bay windows lashed with sea-spray,
'I'll always hold a candle,' she would say &
I think how love is like a shining ruby,
while tides drift, sunlight fades.

Tasseography

For my Dapir

She holds the teacup to her lips,
gold-rimmed, a protective eye of tea leaves,
cardamom swirling, a caldera
of hidden depths; divination in the debris.

Honey-drenched, rose-scented,
stories run through my mind like sepia,
her voice dark like tea as it steeps.
Her face is cast bronze by a veil of light
shining through the lace curtains.

She cries into the brew, tells of her troubled eyes a
reckoning of tears. What her eyes have witnessed.

There are quiet moments like these,
where tea soothes and there is nothing left to do
but listen, sit, sip together,
watch mountains bloom and tides change
in our teacups.

NAZAND BEGIKHANI

The War Was Over

Christmas Day
I arrived at my mother's house
with my four-year-old son
That was their first encounter

My son had seen her photographs
and jumped into her arms
My mother was struggling to hide her tears

No one will know
if they were tears of joy
or of grief for the loss of my brother
who carried the same name

In deep silence
still in her arms
Nawzad smiled and said:
I have missed you Nana giyan

A Child's Painting

On a drawing by my three-year-old son

A blue line
is bending
it turns towards you
an arrow facing the south
what does it tell you, mother?

My life is full of circles
and they are intermingled
a black point in the centre
tells of departure

All signs bend towards you
to the early days
the colours of the lines are magic
my smile is bright
in the arms of you mother
and you father

The blue line is life
when my father climbed up
nothing happened
when you wanted to climb higher
into your own life
I was alone, mother

CHOMAN HARDI

Excerpt from *Whispering Walls*

The Photographs

Hiwa sighed. He switched off the TV and looked out from the sitting room window for a long time. A fine rain was falling, a monotonous and soundless beat which reminded him once again that he was away from his homeland. Back there, raindrops rapidly hit the ground and flooded the gardens and roads. Back there, there were definite seasons, frosty winters, scorching summers, a few months of green and a few months of gold. The carpets were unrolled and laid out for the winter and packed away for the summer. The fruit and vegetables were seasonal. All the colours, tastes and smells used to remind him which season he lived in.

Hiwa felt grateful that his wife was not there to see him take his time. He passed by the large mirror in the corridor and stopped to have a look. His black hair was growing too long, and his beard was three days old. His large brown eyes were lively, they brightened up his face. He rubbed his chin and remembered his wife's complaint the night before.

'You are stinging me,' she said while gently stroking his head.

'I love stinging you,' he told her.

He walked away from the mirror whistling an old Kurdish song, 'I want a kiss right now / I won't leave it till midnight'.

It was 10 a.m. on Saturday morning, 1 February 2003. Hiwa opened the door to 'the study' and stood in the door frame. He looked at the bookshelves, the boxes, and the book piles all over the floor. In a distant land, seas, fields, and mountains away his dead siblings stirred in their graves. Kawa's large blue eyes smiled, and Tara sat up in anticipation. They had been waiting for this moment for many years. They were holding their breath.

'Go on,' Hiwa thought he heard Tara whisper encouragingly, 'Free us.'

He stepped forward, picked up the first large box, and brought it to the middle of the room before putting it down and opening it. All the things that were waiting to be released prepared to stretch their wings.

∴

Outside the evening was dark like ink. The rain had stopped but Hiwa felt the dampness in his books and papers. He was starting to realise that clearing 'the study' would take longer than he had planned. He'd spent the weekend, including most evenings, among the scraps of paper, photos and tapes that embodied his past. He was still creating more mess than order.

He sipped his cold tea while scanning the chaos around him. There were separate piles for the different kinds of paper. The largest pile consisted of rubbish: papers, receipts, Christmas cards he didn't know why he had kept, and letters from people whose names he didn't recognise anymore.

There was an urge in him to keep things in case they would become important one day. He used to have a similar problem with his clothes. His cupboard kept getting more crammed, but he could not bring himself to throw anything away. It took Sarah, the woman who later broke his heart, an entire year before she persuaded him to give up his old shirts and trousers to the charity shop.

Hiwa's mother didn't throw things away, she kept recycling them. Ahoo used the wool from old jumpers to knit new ones. Shirts and dresses were passed down the family, altered for the younger children. Old sheets and leftover cloths were cut into square pieces and sewn together to make patchwork quilts. Hiwa missed sleeping in the heavy quilts, the love that went into making them made them cosier.

Sozi and Shilana were in the bathroom. Hiwa heard his daughter giggle as she played in the lukewarm bath. He knew that she was surrounded by her ducks and bubbles.

'Yuck,' Sozi told her daughter, 'You can't eat that, it is dirty.'

Hiwa loved children's open minds about things, how they wanted to experience everything, touching and tasting indiscriminately. Sometimes he realised that a dog was barking outside only when his daughter said 'wa waw.' She was alert to all the sounds he had become accustomed to, and he wished she would maintain her freshness.

He stopped shovelling through his papers to look at family photographs harvested from various envelopes and boxes. There was a picture of the women of the family smiling at him. Hiwa guessed that his brother, Rizgar, must have taken the photograph. It was dated 2nd of July 1992, two years after Kawa's death and the year his mother would die. The women were still wearing black for Kawa.

His mother was in the centre of the photograph. Sitting on the floor, Ahoo had a tray of tea glasses and saucers, a pot of steaming tea, and the sugar box in front of her. She was wearing her traditional clothes—black dress, black waistcoat, and black undergarments. Her thin white scarf could not tame her bulky hair, it stood stiffly.

The younger women were huddled around Ahoo. On her right Lana was smiling, leaning on her mother's shoulder, in black pyjamas. Kawa's widow, Aveen, was sitting next to Lana wearing a black night gown. She was all covered up, her hair tied in a ponytail and her legs tucked under her body. She was looking at the camera with a faint smile. On the left his aunt, Seyran, was waving at the camera. She looked pale but was smiling. Her navy gown looked too big for her. Hiwa could not remember whether her rheumatism had already flared up by that time, but her handwriting was shaky at the back of the photograph: 'Hiwa gian, we miss you very much and hope that you will be able to visit soon. We pray for your health and happiness.'

Ahoo was the only one who looked happy in the picture, her teeth showing as she smiled. She was the one who would die soon and Hiwa wondered whether the others already knew this at the time. It felt like a landmark picture taken to remember the spirit of Ahoo, sitting cross-legged by the steaming *semawer* and pouring tea for everyone.

His mother's sweet tea was perfumed with the right amount of cardamom and cinnamon. Hiwa had never since drunk tea that tasted so good. Even when Sozi and Lana used the same recipe it was never the same. He was convinced that people poured a bit of themselves into the things they made. Some people could not cook, not because they did not know how but because that bit of themselves which they put into their cooking was not right.

All his life he had searched for a woman who was not only lovely in herself but also in the things she touched, made, cooked. That was why Sozi had occupied his life so quickly. She could transform a room, making slight alterations. She could cook in a rush and make the most basic ingredients taste good. He imagined the best ingredient came from her daring vision, the sweat of her hand, the spray of her breath.

Hiwa looked for a space to separate this picture from the rest. He stood up and cleared a small corner at the edge of his computer desk. He put the photograph down, facing upwards, and stood there inspecting it for a second before going back to his piles on the floor.

Shilana was yelling in the other room. She did not like being dried and clothed. This was her cue that it was bedtime.

'Babah,' she called to him crying, 'babababa.'

Hiwa was tempted to respond to her cries, to go and rescue her from this oppression. He often felt like giving in to his daughter who appealed to him for help at times of crisis, urging him to side with her against her mother. He tried hard to stay out of these conflicts.

Hiwa flicked through more pictures. There were childhood photographs of all of them, some too blurred to be recognisable. A photo of Kawa in shorts jumped out at him. Kawa's knees were scabby. He was staring into the camera with his clear blue eyes, one hand on the mud-brick courtyard wall. The photograph had been taken just before Ahoo banned him from standing by the wall. After seeing the holes on the wall increase, she started watching him and soon realised what the problem was.

Every time Ahoo caught her middle son pretending to play by the wall she would give chase, but she was never able to catch him. Kawa would run as fast as he could and spend the whole day hiding until his mother pretended to have forgotten. She knew that if she did not let it go he wouldn't reappear for days. Gradually it seemed as if she didn't notice his clay-eating habit anymore, or maybe she just gave up fighting him.

Hiwa searched his mind for an image of the road where he lived his youth. Had he known how much he would miss the dusty roads and golden twilights he would have paid more attention to the daily details—the bumps in the ground that tripped him up, the stones that lay at rest until a child turned them over, the bright light which made the mud-brick walls paler, the cracks that crept up on houses, the sweet honeysuckle drooping from the walls.

Every morning, long after his father had gone to his bakery, Hiwa got up after several calls from Ahoo. He sat around the *sifra* with his siblings and gobbled up the warm bread, sour yogurt, and sweet tea. He then left home, turned left to the bottom of their dirt road, and then left again onto the street. The narrow road was always buzzing with its small shops, the public hammams with their domed tops (one for men and another for women and children), and the small mosque which was drenched in blue and inscribed with holy words.

The women endlessly haggled with the stubborn and experienced shopkeepers over the price of meat, vegetables, dry food, spices, clothes, and gold. Some of them were wearing an abba which covered them from top to toe, others walked around in their 'modern' clothing. He remembered the way men turned their heads to watch the women pass. One of his father's friends had once told him that men turn around to look at women because women were the suns and men were the sunflowers.

The shop owners sat on their small stools in their traditional dress and headwear. They saw to their customers in between entertaining their guests—old men who moved about slowly, leaning on their walking sticks. They sat by the heater with their coats on during the winter, and in the summer they sat at the edge of the shop, sweating and drinking iced water from a thermos. Sometimes they teased the children, asked them who their parents were, and told them funny stories about their father or mother when they were kids.

At twilight, when fathers came home, the road was filled with the smell of food, the sizzling oil, fried onion, and most of all the aroma of rice topped with meat, almonds, and raisons. Little was left from those hundreds of walks that took Hiwa from home to the outside world and back. He had never thought that one day he would be ripped away from that place, those meals, the togetherness of his family, the ordinariness of life, and the simple daily routines. He had thought that life would remain straightforward, that his siblings would grow old around him, and that their house would remain uncontaminated.

Sometimes the smell of honeysuckle or a spray of dust in the wind would take him back to those days. He would stop in his place, close his eyes, and briskly relive those moments. He longed for that period before his father's accident, before Tara's suicide, before Kawa's murder and his mother's decline from grief. Maybe he longed for his innocence, for the seasonal routines that grounded his experience of home.

He regretted not remembering the details of his mother's face. He had not looked at her properly all those mornings when she poured him tea and gave him warm bread before he left the house. He could not remember their conversations at breakfast, lunch, and dinner. He could not remember what he had thought and felt at the end of the seasons. And worst of all, no new experience could match that of those days, nothing was as rich in colour, taste, and smell as the memories of that poor road. It was as if with the loss of that life his senses were numbed. He could not feel the same excitement and enthusiasm about anything anymore. All of Europe with its lush landscape, seas, and mountains could not make him feel as he had done all those years ago.

'Maybe it was because I was young' he regularly thought, 'Or maybe this is what displacement does to your senses, it dulls and dilutes your experiences of the world.'

The photographs were colourful windows to another world, crystallised moments in a family history. They sparkled at certain angles, reflecting so much light that the image disappeared. Hiwa decided to organise them in a chronological order. He imagined his daughter looking at these photos one day, imagined telling her stories about her aunts and uncles. He contemplated the only photo he had brought with him. He had carried the black-and-white photograph of Tara in his wallet as he crossed the mountains to Iran, guided by smugglers. From Iran he had gone to Syria, and from there he had flown to London.

Throughout his journey to the UK, he had repeatedly taken the photograph out of his wallet and looked at it. Once he was teased by a young man who accompanied him for a part of the way. Hiwa sighed in response and left his co-traveller to imagine all sorts of stories about this beautiful woman. Tara must have been fifteen in the picture. Her full lips looked pale; her green eyes were light grey. Her long black hair was loose. She was smiling faintly, a smile so small that it could be missed in haste. He tried to imagine what she would look like if she had been alive. He pursed his lips.

Hiwa's finger traced the edge of the small picture, which was now marked, with tiny white lines running through its surface. He got up once more and put the photograph on top of the other at the edge of the desk. He was bent down surveying her face again when he heard his daughter rapidly approach the room with tiny footsteps. She came in, her hair was loose and wet from the bath, she was wearing her green pyjamas and her big eyes looked greener than usual. She stood for a second inspecting the papers and calculating what she should attack first.

Hiwa looked at her, as if for the first time. He jumped backwards in shock. He suddenly realised who she looked like. He rushed towards her and picked her up midair just before she jumped on his photographs.

'Dear God!' he said while holding her close to his chest, 'Oh dear God!'

PINAR BANU YAŞAR

Past and Future Selves Consider Language

what is the word for / gun / *what is the word for* / we should break up because after graduation i am moving / towards myself finally / and you call that shortsighted / *what is the word for* / how can it be shortsighted to defend my family's land / how can you be the love in my hands when your words wrestle me down like i am dirt and you are the worm here to toss me about for my own good / to feed everyone else / to feed yourself / *what is the word for* / even my father understands / *what is the word for* / seeing the possibility of yourself in someone else / *what is the word for* / teach me how to shoot like my grandfather / *what is the word for* / fear / they run from us because to be killed by a woman is to forsake those fabled virgins / for once / my womanhood / is a weapon not turned on me / it is the wolf that protects the land / *what is the word for* / hello / i love you / i am like you / i am still learning how to die / i am still drowning in another language but i am learning how to hold my breath until we meet again / *what is the word for* / bone / mountain / i know they are the same / in our bodies / *what is the word for* / a haunting i ask for / *what is the word for* / ancestral habits / *what is the word for* / after graduation i am moving towards myself finally and you call that shortsighted but i will defend my family's land i am learning how to shoot like my grandfather with the weapon that is my womanhood and the words that foam against my wolfish teeth hello i love you i am like you i am still learning how to / *what is the word for* / diaspora / *what is the word for* / escape / *what is the word for* / let go / *what is the word for* / return / *what is the word for* / the diaspora was our escape but i cannot let go so i will return / *what is the word for* / do you recognize me / yet / *what is the word for* / i am moving towards myself i will defend my family's land i have learned how to shoot and i have always been a wolf hello i love you always and in all ways because nothing / not the ocean / not this language / not this country / can stop me from / coming home

The Relevant Parties

Kill me! But you must also know that after my death thousands of Kurds will wake up.
—LEYLA QASIM

i.

means they have the ears of heaven folded /
they are calling genocide a bookmark and
God's absence a statement / a
miscommunication / "all people, my people"
/ my people, your people / is not bread a
history? / is not flour unsifted possibilities?

ii.

I say Iranian because we are taught that in
order to belong we need a country to return
to, which is not always the same as the
country you are from, and this is one way I
am taught to record, attempts to belong in
the ranks of those keeping track, it never
makes much difference to the white
imagination that I am light-skinned for a Kurd,
I am a foreigner either way in America,
I say Iranian because in order to belong
you need a country to return me to.

iii.

a well / a forest / a mirror to only
those who have never seen a colonizer before.

iv.

headline:

"Father shot dead, son wounded for saying 'we are Kurds' in Turkey"

reddit comment:

"No one cares about your family you

stupid piece of shit"

my neighbor:

"You're next"

v.

means I have made it past twenty-two

without tasting prison food,

my father still hasn't told me the name

of that fruit

but i can hear it crunching,

snapping off in his hands,

in a place i can never return to.

vi.

my crimes are many.

i am alive.

i am alive.

i am alive.

i am alive.

vii.

are they dragging me onto the pavement

am i running, running red, running from

death? i am still learning how to,

a tree sprouts in my palm,

growing bountiful countries

none I may touch without being burned,

for linguicide to succeed I must

plant the tree and watch it die,

agonize over what fed, what drank,

what failed in me

viii.

I say Iraqi because in order to be returned

I have to return to the right place and there is

no right place so I reach back into the roots

and trace the next one, hoping this one

won't dry out like the last, to the white imagination

I am still a flightless bird changing flight pattern,

hobbling below my brothers and sisters,

pointing to the sky and making shallow graves in the clouds

for each word that gets lost in translation

MERYEM RABIA UZUMCU

Family Rashomon

A personal narrative on the difference between two members of a family who experienced migration to the US differently, based on intergenerational and linguistic gaps. The first-generation American experience and the immigrant parent experience is explored by Meryem Rabia Uzumcu.

Meryem: Hibiscus flowers with bright fuchsia stamens, my brother's eyes glued to *Crash Bandicoot* on his PlayStation 1, and Assad's treacherous deployment of rainbow BB pellets on the Al-Maroosh compound paint my first childhood memories. And in the backdrop is probably my sister singing along to Christina Aguilera's "Genie in a Bottle." Long days of playing in the hot Saudi sunshine were never interrupted by snow or rain. The compound walls gated the outside world from our meadowy utopia equipped with a pool. What more could I ask for? But life in Saudi Arabia was different for my mother.

Mother: Saudi Arabia was hard for me. I feel that I [was] kind of in prison.

Meryem: Granted, being a child is very different from being a grown woman in Saudi. But sometimes, it feels like this apple (me) fell in a completely different country from its tree.

Mother: I [was] born in Diyarbakır, Turkey . . .

Meryem: For first-gens like my siblings and I, there's not only a generational gap, but a cultural difference from our parents. After Saudi, when we moved to Washington, these girls on the bus gave me these Britney Spears cards, and her belly was showing, and then I showed them to you, and you made me rip them up and said, "You're not like those girls."

Mother: Yeah I don't remember, but probably I did it.

Meryem: My mom always tried to insert her values into our upbringing, and sometimes we really saw the world differently than one another.

Mother: You have your own culture, you have your own saturations, you have your own beliefs. You just wanna keep it. [Arabic music plays in the background]

Meryem: To do this interview with my mom, we went to Rutgers gardens at our alma mater's campus. She graduated in 2006 when she was forty-six, and I almost ten years later in 2017. Every spring, we smell our way through this flowery passageway formed by the lilac trees' first bloom in mid-April.

Mother: This is, little corner of the heaven, kind of. It's so beautiful.

Meryem: The hum of Highway Route 18 is in the background. And even if it smells like heaven, we're still in New Jersey.

Mother: Ah, it smells strong too. I'm speechless.

Meryem: She's speechless, which is the opposite effect I want the interview to have. So we move away from the magical waft of pink and purple lilacs and toward the gazebo. [Her mother sits and sighs] It took me a long time to understand her reasoning that told me to rip up the Britney Spears cards.

Mother: Maybe you understand now, but maybe not that time.

Meryem: For a long time I thought she was doing it because she didn't get America. Most immigrants relate to America through the cliché of the American dream. I wondered what my mom thought of her own immigrant experience. Why did you move to the United States?

Mother: My husband got a scholarship to come to the US to do his PhD. And we moved. So I stopped working, I stopped my education to come to the United States. When I came here with a baby, I didn't have any language skills.

Meryem: My mom took an almost ten-year break from school to learn a new language and raise three children. Meanwhile, she was following her husband's career around the world, which is how we ended up in Saudi Arabia in the first place. When we moved to New Jersey, my mom enrolled at Rutgers.

Mother: My journey started in college with the three kids. If there is a will, there's a way. I believe in that, and I never underestimated the small things that I achieved. I go forward and that's it. I just think what I am going to do in my life.

Reynolds: Your mother is very goal oriented. That's the impression I got, she has a sense of direction and she's going in that direction, and she is very serious.

Meryem: That's Rebecca Reynolds, she's a dean at Rutgers University.

Reynolds: And she wanted to figure out how she could register for classes.

Meryem: With her help, my mother was able to graduate with a bachelor's degree in public health, and it didn't stop there.

Mother: I want to become a physical therapist, I don't know why. Maybe because I have personal injury in the back, but the operational therapy suited me more. I was searching what school fits me more, and I found that Columbia is a good option. I said, you know, "I'm going to apply to this school and see what happens."

Meryem: Considering all of her challenges along the way, my mother completed her second degree in occupational therapy at an Ivy League school. I still wonder if she related to the ultimate cultural cliché. Do you feel like you have achieved the American dream?

Mother: People come to the United States for opportunity, but I had everything in my country. My story is a very opposite one. I left my dreams. I received support later on, you know, people like me around me, and from Turkey people sending me letters all the time. When I went to check my mailbox I found five letters, so I was happy that day.

Meryem: The truth is, it's hard to pin anyone down to simple clichés. Turkey was this faraway place that was still intimate and important for us to recognize in terms of language, culture, and most of all, values.

Mother: I never think that I can totally erase my culture. This country is a totally different cultures, combinations, everyone in their home, they're living their own culture.

Meryem: To my mom, American culture was not about assimilation but establishing her own values here, and having the freedom to do that.

Mother: Being different is not too bad that I made the space, sometimes it's a positive thing actually for society. I think it takes time until you get your confidence and you know what you're doing, and then you say, "Oh okay, it can be like this way too."

Meryem: And at home, she enforced that being different—our culture—was the norm.

Mother: When everyone else is against you, I feel stronger. [laughter from both]

Meryem: Growing up, I thought my mom's values were a little overbearing. Until I went to college and entered the real world, and unless you actually stand up for yourself, life is hard. My mom was standing up for her way of thinking and doing things while raising us. American or Turkish, her values reflected a life striving for self-actualization.

Meryem: Do you think we understand each other now?

Mother: I think so. How about you?

Meryem: I think I understand you.

Mother: You understand me?

Meryem: I think, I don't know.

Mother: You think I understand you?

Meryem: Do you think you understand me?

Mother: No, do you feel that way? [laughs]

Meryem: I'm just asking you.

Mother: Yeah, I feel that way, yeah I understand you. [both laugh] Now I'm asking you questions.

Meryem: In that moment, we were like two kids bashfully asking each other if the other would be her friend.

ROOZ MOHAMMED

Pages from the graphic novel *Between Two Rivers*

—Translated from the Kurdish (Sorani) by Halo Fariq and Hannah Fox

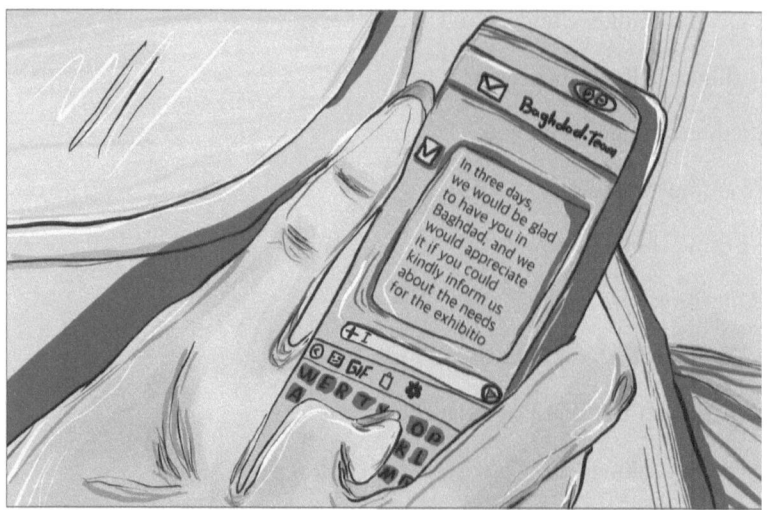

A message arrives that keeps me from listening.

The word Baghdad in my memory is this picture with my father.
I wonder what Baghdad is like now?

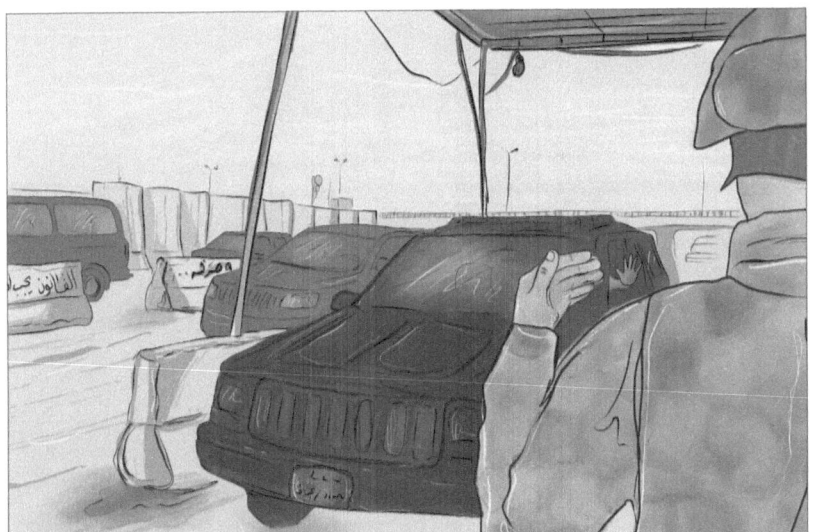

I want to enjoy the nice side of the city, but I can't look away from all the checkpoints in the middle of the streets, which look like iron tents. *They give me an ironic feeling: I don't know whether they protect me, or frighten me.*

In this scene, my eyes fall on a pair of red shoes, which sometimes appear under the darkness of an abaya. *The inside of this city seems to be brighter than it first appears.*

After twenty-two years, I return to the place where a photo was taken of me as a child. This time, I'm grown up and my father is not accompanying me. This is the first time I feel a sense of my own aging. I think about my body—how much has changed! I raise my head to look at the bodies of the figures on the wall and think: *Are these also the bodies of Iraqi citizens?*

I am happy with their love for life, but the way they stare reminds me of the stares I received one afternoon in Saholaka when I cut my hair short for the first time. As I passed by, their looks were digging into my skin like nails. I wanted to scream, "IS IT MY BODY OR YOURS?"

Rooz Mohammed

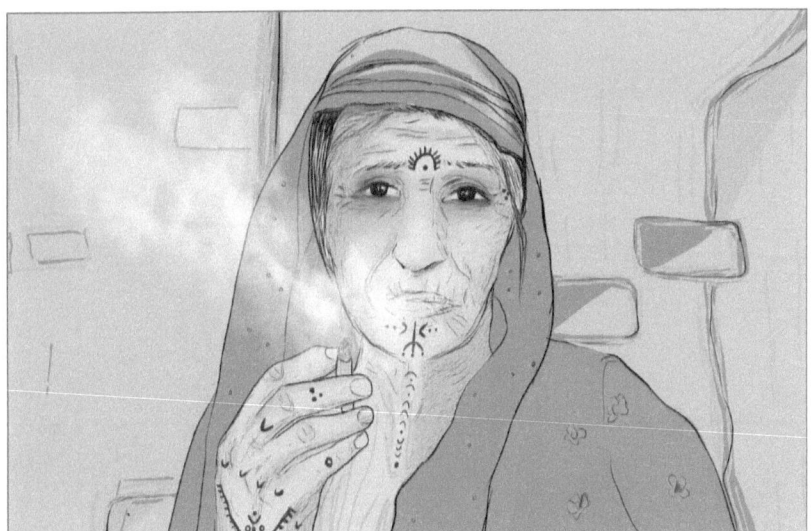

Her tattoos and the kohl marking her eyes reveal a beauty that is pouring from between the two rivers. *This kind woman, with her tattoos and her half-smoked cigarette between her fingers, shows a kind of beauty that has become shameful nowadays, but I don't know why!*

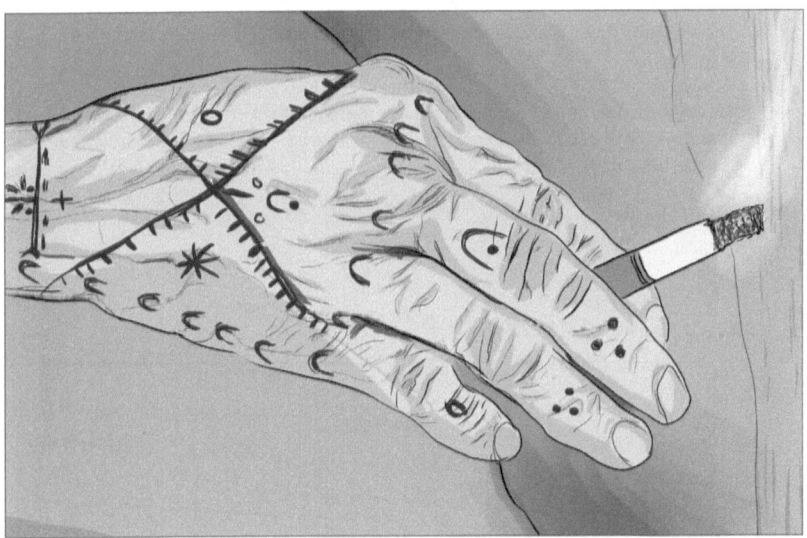

The wrinkles under her tattoos are a sign from an era where we were the owner of our own decisions and the body belonged to individuals. Making marks and tattoos on the skin was a traditional culture in this place, but it was ended and made into a shameful act. *Was it because this culture was a sign of women's freedom?*

Returning

I believe that we can't return from a place without leaving a part of ourselves there. I return with more memories and questions than I can talk about. From the air, I look down at the land between the two rivers. Do I understand where Baghdad is?

I open the front door of our house, in a hurry to get to my room and write my memories of Baghdad. I hear my parents. My mother calls me, "Come downstairs! Tell us, how was it?"

Rooz Mohammed

ESSMAT SOPHIE

Setar on the Mud Wall

Since the day I went to see Minoo after Sima's funeral, she has often come to my dreams. Although the details of my dreams are different every time, Minoo is always young in them. Her thyroid gland is not bulging out of her neck, and her jet-black hair has covered her neck and shoulders; the skin under her eyes is not puffy either. In my dreams, I am my current age. The dream is generally the same: Minoo is standing on the stage of a giant hall, singing. Behind her, tar, dulcimer, and daf players are sitting in a row.[1] Minoo is standing, and I sit somewhere far from her, listening to her. In some dreams I'm slightly closer, able to see her bulging eyes. Her hands, her voice, and even her head are trembling. She used to tie a floral velvet *sarband* to her Kurdish scarf and set it dancing with her trembling head.[2] I become worried and ask, "Why are you trembling? Your eyes?" She laughs and says, "Don't worry, it is alright. Everything is going to be alright very soon."

Recently I wanted to get closer to her in my dreams, but just at the moment I'm about to hold her hand, a huge crowd rushes toward her, raises her above their heads, and takes her away.

After the funeral, I went home. I picked up a package I had made before and took a taxi to Minoo's house. The taxi driver was listening to a sad song by

1. The tar is an Iranian-Kurdish long-necked, waisted instrument, shared by many cultures and countries including Kurdistan, Iran, Azerbaijan, Armenia, Georgia, and others near the Caucasus region. The word *tār* means "string" in Persian, and it is also related to the names of the guitar, sitar, *setar* (three strings), and *dutar* (two strings). The daf is a large Middle Eastern frame drum used in popular and classical music. The frame is usually made of hardwood with many metal ringlets attached. The membrane is usually fish skin, but other skin types such as cow, goat, and horse are also used.

2. Hair decorating string for women. They decorate their hair with dangling coins and jewels. It can be a traditional head covering in this region that is very similar to the *kalāǧī*, a cap decorated with sequins and wrapped with one or two scarves.

Kurdish singer Hama Jaza. Hearing that sad music, especially after the funeral, in addition to the driver's cigarette smoke blowing directly into my face in that hot weather, frustrated me. Instead of turning on the AC, the driver had rolled down his window. As I inhaled, my lungs burned with car exhaust and acrid cigarette smoke. The taxi stopped in front of a new brick building that sat behind a fence made from stone and wrought iron. A sign with silver *nasta'liq* calligraphy letters appeared on the main entrance.[3] I read the sign: "Social Security Office, Region 3." The taxi driver, who looked about forty-five with grayish hair and a goatee, threw his cigarette butt out the window, rolled it up a bit, adjusted the mirror to reflect my face, and announced in a hoarse croak that the road was dirt from now on and he couldn't drive on a dirt road with so many bumps. I wanted to object and ask why he didn't say it when I gave him the address, but his sullen, serious, sweaty, and tired face, which looked like he was ready for cursing and fighting at any second, made me give up. It was hot, and walking on a hot dirt road at 4:30 in the afternoon was no fun. It wasn't even a good time for recollection in those dirt alleys, which looked so modern with new buildings but were not asphalted yet, and I had memories of each and every one of them. I would have to walk the rest of the way. I left the taxi and headed to the hill.

At my left, where the Ardalan family's big mansion used to be years ago, now stood a newly built mosque with *chartaq* architecture and an exterior decorated with plasterwork, mirror decorations, and turquoise tiles.[4] In front of the mosque was a small round pool containing a fountain. Watching water falling from the fountain and the turquoise tiles of the mosque made me feel cooler in that hot weather.

I turned into a narrow alley at the right side of the mosque. At the end of it was Golchin alley, where Minoo's house and my childhood home were located. From all the trees I had known there, only a few willows and oaks remained. In the slight incline of the alley, there was no sign of our home. In its place, a new multistory apartment building with silver windows had been built. Slightly further, instead of Minoo's big family house there now stood a new apartment building with small balconies and big windows. A few years ago, they had to sell their

3. *Nasta'liq* is one of the main calligraphic handwriting styles used in Persian script, and traditionally the predominant style in Persian calligraphy.
4. *Chartaq*, literally meaning "four arches," is an architectural unit consisting of four barrel vaults and a dome.

home and move to an old, tiny cob house at the end of the alley and the beginning of the hill. The cob house with its weathered wooden door, perched between the modern and new buildings of the alley, looked like the type of mysterious, ancient house that falls to ruin and then is combed for treasures in tales and films. I started going uphill, and when I reached the front of the cob house, I was out of breath. From the corner of the half-closed door, I took a glance inside; no one was in the yard. I searched for a doorbell but couldn't find one. Instead, I rapped three times with a ring built into the old wooden door and waited . . . no answer. Knocked again. This time, I saw through the corner of the door Hosein Khan, Minoo's father, resting his head on the window and looking at me. I waited for him to come to the yard. He wore gray striped pajamas and a light summer shirt. His body looked weaker and more fragile than last time.

I said hello. He looked at me for a bit. I asked, "You don't remember me, do you?" He brushed back his thin, messy hair with his trembling hand, stroked his white beard, and looked again. "If you stand further back," he said, "I can recognize your face. I can't see clearly up close." Dragging his loose navy-blue slippers, he went back a few steps. I did the same. Then he recognized me, smiled, and in a whistling voice said, "I know you, butt-burned brat." I laughed, went forward, and kissed his trembling hands. He called me that when I was a kid. Once, at Chaharshanbe Suri, while jumping over the fire, I burned my long red dress—which had white flowers and which I had just received as a new year's present from him—right on the bottom.[5] From then on, he called me by that nickname. He gave me piggyback rides so many times as a kid, and in those years I always thought that he was the strongest and bulkiest man I knew. And it was true. My father and other friends as old as Hosein Khan had died years ago, but at eighty-five, he was able not only to handle his own affairs but also to take care of Minoo.

He put his trembling, bony fingers on my shoulders and showed me into the house. We passed through the small doorway, entering a narrow hallway and then the living room. A dim glow from two windows covered with white curtains lit the living room and cob walls. In that pale light, I saw Minoo by the opposite wall lying on the ground on a brown floral blanket, her right hand hanging from a cushion by the wall. On her left was an ashtray full of cigarette butts and a

---

5. Chaharshanbe Suri is the Kurdish-Persian Festival of Fire, celebrated on the eve of the last Wednesday before Nowruz (the Kurdish-Iranian new year).

glass of tea. Her eyes were open, seemingly staring at a *setar* and a *daf* hanging on the worn wall in front of her.

She wasn't aware of our presence. At the left edge of the room, there was an old, small, green couch on which a pile of pills and other medications rested.

Hosein Khan guided me to the couch and went to the other side of the room, which was separated by a curtain from the rest of the house, to bring me water from their kitchenette. I put my handbag by the couch. On the niche on the wall by my side were framed pictures of young Minoo. Minoo with beautiful Kurdish clothes and a *sarband* embroidered with velvet flowers, Minoo playing a *tar*, Minoo and Master Valiollah Adib. The Minoo in the pictures was the one I knew, but I had to turn back to the one lying on the brown floral blanket.

I went to her. She still wasn't aware of my presence. I held her hand in mine. She turned and looked at me, and a shy smile came to her lips. I helped her sit up. She brushed her white hair away from her forehead. The big thyroid gland under her neck, bigger than before, bulged out from under her scarf. She kept holding my hand and smiled again. Her skinny, long fingers were trembling in mine. I knew she didn't remember me. I told her that I had brought her a gift, something she liked a lot: a traditional Kurdish dress. I said, "Get up, Minoo. Put this on and see how well it fits you."

I helped her stand up from her blanket. Her back seemed a bit more bent than before. With a glance, I saw our image in a little mirror on the wall, and I noticed that even with that slightly hunched back, she was still a few inches taller than me. She smiled at her image.

I sat her on the couch and put the dress on her. It was very hot inside; a fan was working on the other side of the room but couldn't fight the heat, and although Hosein Khan brought me cold water, sweat was still dripping from my body. When I finished dressing her up with new clothes, she held my hand and dragged me to the mirror. Adjusting the *sarband* on her head, she stuttered, smiling: "She's pretty, tall, has a pretty face, she's pretty, very amazing voice, very famous, very pretty, these clothes become her well." Like the last time, she talked about herself in the third person. I said, "Dear Minoo, clothes suit you well, of course you're so pretty. And your beauty is amazing."

It was after that day, after Sima's funeral, when I went to visit Minoo, that I started to dream about her often. Sometimes Sima was also in the dreams. Sima and Minoo, at the same age that we used to go to Master Valiollah Adib's tar class together, exactly like those days when we used to wait by the window for Minoo's father to take us to the class. But in these dreams, I, on the other hand, am always the age as I am now.

It was exactly four months ago, in early June, the night we were busy getting prepared for my oldest son's wedding and were all excited for the event, when my phone rang. It was Sima's husband from France. He said that Sima was in the hospital and wanted to talk to me. I didn't call her for a while; I knew that she was ill but didn't want to believe it and postponed calling her. That night, Sima's voice on the phone was croaky, as if she had a cold or maybe a stuffy nose from crying. She tried to send her humor and high spirits from the other side of the line, saying she finally wanted to go back to Sanandaj real soon. She asked me to plan the summer vacation to go back to Kurdistan together. I asked her if she was worried that there had been a problem. "It has been years now since your records and voice were banned in that country, maybe they will trouble you if you go back." She laughed and said that at her age no one cares about her. "I don't want to sing in Iran! I want to be together like in our childhood days again." She also talked about Minoo, wanting to be closer to her, too. Before saying goodbye, she laughed and said, "So long then! See you in Kurdistan."

Which came true. Two weeks after that conversation, Sima passed away and, in accordance with her will, her body was returned to her birthplace for burial. I came back from Sweden to Iran, still engaged in final planning and preparation for my son's wedding, to attend Sima's funeral. My famous hometown singer and dear childhood and adulthood friend.

On the day of the funeral, the crowd was so huge that all main roads to the graveyard were closed. Even in the main boulevard entrance to the graveyard lines of people blackened the whole street. All celebrity artists, all writers, and the city's nobles were there. The ceremony, including eulogies and speeches, took three hours. Even Mr. Hooshang, who Sima, Minoo, and I were all repelled by for years, was there with his cane, and he gave a speech in memory of Sima, closing it by emphasizing her grave as an honor for the city that will shine there forever like a work of art. It wasn't just Mr. Hooshang, who always declared in his speeches and writings that female singers were whores, that Sima and I hid our voices from for years. Most of the people who attended the funeral backbit her for years as an iconoclast singer, wrote articles against her, and called her a depraved tramp. But now they considered her body a priceless gem for the city, a gem decorating their patriotism.

Apart from Saaderat's bank manager, no one from city hall or other governmental authorities attended. After the Islamic Revolution, the female voice was banned in Iran. As someone who had crossed the red line and broken a taboo, Sima, through exclusion and disregard, was punished even after death.

That day, after the funeral, in the midst of the greetings and attention of old friends and acquaintances, I went to Minoo's home. I knew visiting her in that physical and mental situation wouldn't be a relief from my grief at losing Sima, but would make it heavier. However, either for unconscious reasons or out of duty, I had to visit her.

Minoo, Sima, and I shared the same age, neighborhood, and school, and our parents were friends. The three of us used to see each other seven days a week; I was either at their houses or they were at mine. Our alley, then called Shams, was at the beginning of a steep road in the Charbagh district. Our house was at the end of the alley, while Minoo's was right at the top, with a green gate and big windows facing the landscape of Abidar mountain and overlooking the lower neighborhood and plain in front. A small spring flowed out of the mountain near the alley and made a tiny stream bordering it. Along its side, willow, oak, and sycamore covered the whole road.

The three of us used to play in the spring and summer afternoons beside the stream and between the trees. Later on when we became older, Minoo's father took us twice a week to tar and singing classes. Those two days, we used to wait by the living room window in Minoo's house for Hosein Khan to arrive, peeking through the window to the yard door, waiting with excitement. While we waited, we'd either gaze at Abidar's beautiful scenery, follow the trail of climbers, or peer up at sparrows' nests above the trees. We could see both the foothills and the peak of Abidar from all the rooms and the yard as well. The windows on the right-hand side of the living room and kitchen opened up to the mountain, and the ones on the left to the plain in front and the lower neighborhood. I don't know why whenever we looked at the mountain that we'd start to fantasize about the future and talk about our plans. Watching the peak and foothills of Abidar and the climbers was pleasant in every season. In spring, the whole plain was covered with poppies, marshmallow flowers, irises, and chamomile, while mulberry trees and plum blossoms decorated most of the way. After the last month of spring, the mountain gradually became khaki in color, but many of the slopes were still covered with trees that looked striped green from a distance. In every season we could see the climbers. But from early fall, when the mountain was a mixture of yellow, orange, and green, then gradually covered by white snow, the line was more visible: a zigzag of figures who, in the early mornings or afternoons, climbed the mountain and looked like a line of ants. Other than Fridays (the weekend), we could see the line every day. Often on early Friday mornings, around 5 a.m., Sima, Minoo, and I used to go climbing with our fathers. We left the house while it was still dark, joined the climbers, and were up on the peak by sunrise. Hosein Khan always brought a small cassette player, and we listened to music all the way up and sang together.

In my family, singing wasn't really acceptable for girls. Sima's father was also against his daughter singing and learning music, but Hosein Khan insisted and persuaded our fathers. Neighbors and acquaintances considered that shameful, outrageous, and breaking the tradition. Every time our neighbor Mr. Hooshang came to our evening gatherings, he used to sarcastically bring up young girls and iconoclasts. Back then, women singing was not customary.

Hosein Khan was from the Ardalan family, and since he was very famous and popular among people, no one could speak against him. He had a great influence on everyone in the neighborhood, not just his friends and acquaintances. It was because of his support that we could attend that music class. Minoo and I played the tar, and Sima played the dulcimer. We also practiced singing with our master. Although Sima and I practiced our music lessons and recited better, he paid more attention to Minoo; he liked her voice and praised her yodeling and the vibrato it had. We accepted that Minoo was his favorite student. Our master was an old friend of Hosein Khan, and maybe this friendship wasn't unconnected to his attention. Minoo, apart from her lessons from the master, also learned singing from her father and practiced the tar. When Hosein Khan took us to the master's house, he always used to sit beside him and listen to our practice. He was always attentive to Minoo's hands and her voice. She used to stand while singing; her figure looked taller and slenderer in her Kurdish dress. She used to brush away her thick, black locks from her wide, white forehead while yodeling, adjust her hairpin, close her eyes, and sing:

My heart longs for you
My melancholy mind thinks about you
My drawn, sallow face looks
Bitterly down for you

The songs we sang were in both Kurdish and Farsi, and the lyrics were from classic poets like Rumi, Hafiz, Nali, and Goran. Kurdish folklore poems were chosen by Master Valiollah Adib for us, but Farsi ones were mostly our own choice or Hosein Khan's. The poems were often about sadness or love. Even when singing happy songs, Minoo always used to frown with her thick brows while closing her eyes, which made her face more attractive. I always saw how Hosein Khan stared at his daughter's face with shining eyes. Later, when Minoo performed at her first concerts, she usually tied to her head a *sarband* or *kalaka* decorated all around with long strings of black and white silk and filigree work.[6] Her mom made headscarves and *kalaka* for her and decorated them with colorful tinsel and golden lace. She always had wonderful taste in making *ghatareh*, hanging a line of lira or pahlavi coins on a golden string, and Minoo passed this beautiful *ghatareh* under her chin and hung it on two sides of the *kalaka*.[7] With her *kalaka* and *ghatareh*, her beauty multiplied a hundredfold. I remember that sometimes when we spoke I became so distracted by her beauty that I couldn't understand what she was saying.

Minoo officially started singing before we'd finished high school. For a year or two before that, during the summers she was a presenter at song-request radio program broadcast from Sanandaj and Kermanshah, and she also sang herself. It was there that she met Shahram. He wasn't a permanent employee of the station, just a sound technician and an electrical engineering student. According to what Minoo told us, after seeing her a few times and listening to her voice, he fell in love with her. At first she didn't care, but Shahram gradually won her heart with love letters, and she fell for him. When Shahram came for her hand, Minoo's father, whose dreams were all about his daughter's singing, agreed to their engagement under the condition that they put off the wedding until after her graduation from art school.

That same year, Minoo enrolled in art school in Tehran. Out of the three of us, only she could go to college. She also performed concerts as the first Kurdish female singer in Iran, and her records became popular. She met music masters and sang in other cities with Master Valiollha Adib, with Hosein Khan's support. The release of "Shirin & Farhad," a song composed by Adib featuring Minoo's voice, spread her fame and popularity all around. She was the first Kurdish singer who could break the male spell of art, music, and singing despite taboos in society. Sima and I, on the other hand, could not continue with singing and music. The same year that we finished high school, our suitors appeared. A year after her graduation, her family gave Sima's hand to her cousin who was studying in

---

6. The traditional head covering in this region of Kurdistan, the *kalaka* or *kalāǰī* is a cap decorated with sequins and wrapped with one or two scarves.

7. *Ghatareh* is a type of headdress and hair decorating string for women, covered with dangling coins and jewels.

France. On their engagement day, I met a man from the groom's side who was also studying abroad, and we got married the next year.

Minoo came back home for summer vacation. All three of us now had a fiancé, and we had even more talks and whispers. During this time, Minoo had become famous through her concerts and recordings of two albums. Her voice had an amazing resonance. Everyone in the city talked about her—her beauty and her golden voice. She was so famous that she didn't dare go shopping with us in the bazaar; people everywhere gathered around and admired her.

That summer we saw Minoo very seldom, as she volunteered to teach children who didn't have a school in a village nearby. Every day, her father gave her a ride to the village fifteen kilometers away from the city, and then she would come back in the afternoons before 4 p.m. on the village bus. I remember the day that she came back late. Her father first came to our home and asked for her. He thought maybe she had come to see me or Sima. When they didn't find her, they checked Sima's and some other acquaintances' houses. But no one knew where she was. With his last hope Hosein Khan went to see Shahram, who was staying with a relative in Sanandaj, thinking he might find her there. Shahram joined him and they went to the village, but even there they couldn't find her. Everybody was worried, wondering what had happened to her.

At midnight, Minoo came back home with a disheveled appearance and dusty clothes. She said that somebody was chasing her and she had to come back all the way on foot, before she passed out. She was unconscious for three days, and when she woke up, she didn't give any explanation. She just said that she escaped from somebody and had to walk all the way back in the dark.

No one knows what happened to Minoo that night. Every time Sima and I went to visit her, she didn't tell us anything. Even if she told her father, it remained a mystery, because he never told anybody. Years after that, everyone made up a story based on their imagination about the night that changed Minoo's life forever. However, no one—not even those of us who were her closest friends—ever learned what happened to her.

After two weeks, Minoo gradually became better, and Sima and I visited her for a few hours every day. Once, she was sad and asked for Shahram. The next day, she complained that he didn't visit her anymore and that it was slowly making her crazy. A week after the incident, Shahram suddenly disappeared and no one saw him again. His sudden absence was a huge shock for Minoo. We started seeing strange changes in her. Sometimes her mother asked us to make cookies to keep her busy. But as soon as we entered the kitchen, Minoo wanted us to wash our hands and the baking trays several times in front of her eyes. Even when we wanted to play tar together, she first cleaned it multiple times with a rag and then asked us to wash our hands before touching the instrument. Sometimes she played tar for us and sang:

Oh my flirtatious lover
Oh my handsome,
Playful sweetheart
You are my only nightingale, my only lover
Without you I'm sick, friendless, and alone
Always sad, impatient, and restless

She began a ritual where she would always clean something after singing—washing dishes, for instance, and rinsing them several times. She even counted the times she washed them, and if she lost the count she started over again. When we visited her a few weeks after that, she no longer spoke to us. She just played the tar and sang sad songs or kept busy washing something. Her mother said she couldn't sleep at night. Doctors gave her tranquilizers, but she threw them all in the trash. The doctor told her parents that if her fiancé visited her she'd get better, but Shahram never did.

That fall and winter, Minoo stayed home. She couldn't go back to school for the next semester in that condition, and she became more and more skinny, pale, and sick day by day, in such a way that, whenever Sima and I visited her, we became increasingly concerned. The second week of spring was Sima's wedding; she and her husband went to France. Two months later was mine. I was to go to Tehran with my husband to fly to Sweden. Minoo came to Sima's wedding, but she fainted in the middle of the ceremony and her parents took her home. She didn't come to my wedding. On the day I was leaving the country, she came to the terminal with her mother to see me off.

I remember that day clearly. I was standing beside her on platform 15. The bus conductor opened the door; Mohsen, my husband, was in the front of the line and quickly came to me, took my hands out of hers, and guided me to the bus. I turned back, kissed Minoo again, and went to the bus. Mohsen took my handbag so I could climb the stairs easier. The tickets were in his hand; our seat numbers were 11 and 12. I sat by the window and tried hard to pull open the coarse blue curtain hanging by a thick string. The string had a lot of friction with the fabric, which made it difficult, but I managed to pull it open halfway. Now I could see the crowd lined up to get on the bus and those standing further away, who had come to see others off. Before getting on the bus, I said goodbye to everyone and hugged them, but I wanted to follow Minoo with my eyes up to the last moment before the bus left and wave to her. I stubbornly wanted to record these last memories of being with her in my mind till the last second. I wanted her to show a sign in this last moment, so that I might become hopeful she would regain her health.

I searched for her in the crowd; at first I couldn't find her, but after a few seconds I saw her beside her mom and my mother, looking at the bus. I waved at her, hoping maybe she could see me. Her gaze was on the bus, but she was lost in her thoughts. All the passengers sat down, and the bus was ready to leave. The bus conductor pushed a young street seller from the door. He had a box of Xorosneshan gum and tissues and was crying out selling them.[8] The boy, who wanted to sell a pack of gum at any price, shouted, "Believe me, Ms. Minoo buys the same gum. She always buys Xorosneshan gum." The bus conductor pushed him out of the way and closed the door.

We waved back to all those people who had come to see us off, but Minoo just gazed at the bus like a person lost in a distant memory. All the people, either in the bus or out on the platform, were looking at her. Her coming to the terminal caused such excitement and hubbub, but she didn't see anyone. She seemed like she was surfing around blind alleys that didn't go anywhere.

Shortly after the war between Iran and Iraq, and a year after Sima and I left Iran, the Islamic Revolution happened. Since my husband didn't serve his mandatory military service and would have problems returning to Iran, I also could not return for years. Sima continued singing in France and became famous among Kurds living all across Europe, so after the revolution she couldn't come back to Iran anymore. I, on the other hand, quit singing and music forever. I continued my education in literature and filled my time with writing, reading, and raising kids. I went back to visit Iran years later, when my eldest son was ten. Meeting Minoo after all those years, I was shocked.

I had heard from friends and family that she'd been ill and was getting worse day by day, but what I saw really stunned me. Minoo didn't know anyone anymore. She left the house during the day and wandered around the town singing. Her mother passed away two years after I left Iran; people said it was from a broken heart, grieving over her daughter. Her father—the strong, happy, popular, and

---

8. A famous gum brand in Iran.

famous Hosein Khan—was now a decrepit yet tenderhearted old man still wanting to be Minoo's support and guardian at any price.

When I went to visit Master Valiollah Adib, he talked a lot about Minoo. He told me that she felt good for a month during these years; every day, she used to go to a smoothie store, stand in front, and watch the smoothie guy, who apparently looked a lot like Shahram. During that time she was completely herself, put on nice clothes every day, wore makeup, and stood for hours in front of the store. Then the smoothie guy found another job and didn't come back. Minoo thought she had lost her man again, and she went back to wandering around the town singing. From then on, she never felt good again and didn't remember anybody. Sometimes she left the house and started singing:

Oh my sad heart, why are you restless,
How long will you be waiting for your lover to come?
Don't cry so much, my mournful heart
Don't be so restless for your lover's absence
Why disgrace, why disappear into desert?
Sad love stories are nothing but fairy tales

Now she can't walk around the streets and sing anymore. Her feet can't stand it, or maybe she can't stand people's merciless looks and their poisonous tongues. For years now, the loneliest loving singer in this town, an iconoclast woman, has cringed tiredly in a corner of the house with her loneliness. Years when everyone has forgotten about Minoo. Even I, her childhood friend, couldn't help her. In that town, there are no government or social programs for helping people with those kinds of problems, or if there are any—like the "Social Security Office, Region 3" a few streets down from her house in that pretty building—they can't really do anything for her.

In the last few years, Minoo has become a subject for journalists from time to time. A few years ago, when I went to visit her, I saw some reporters there for an interview. They stood by her side one by one and took pictures as a memento. One of them asked Minoo to hold her old photo in her hands so he could take a picture of her with a portrait of her youth. What a difference! What did the journalist want to prove by showing the contrast between these two pictures, between past and present? So what? Now, instead of her larynx, her hands and head trembled. That damn goiter that covered her whole neck, extremely bulging eyes, her pure white hair, dry wrinkled skin, moles of different sizes all over her face, yellowed teeth with half of them missing, bags under her eyes, her wandering gaze, cigarette in her hand, cracked lips, which one did he want to capture? Which contrast? But Minoo is still beautiful. Her shy smile still sits on her lips. Nevertheless, people like that journalist and I go to see her like an artistic sculpture that has survived wind and rain. But no one can alleviate her pain. Sima and I wished we could, but we couldn't mend this precious creature alone.

When she sat down, she said again: "She's so beautiful, so much. Look how tall she is." She went to the mirror again: "How pretty she has become. This dress suits her a lot."

I looked at her and said, "Yes, dear, you are very beautiful, very graceful . . . these clothes become you."

I held her hand in mine, helped her sit on the couch. I took her pills from a corner and looked at my watch, asked Hosein Khan if it was time for her medication. He nodded yes. I brought a glass of water and gave her the pill. I drew a pack of cigarettes out of my bag and lit one for her. She smiled.

I had to go; I just wanted to pay a short visit and return home. I had come to attend Sima's funeral and check on Minoo and take a picture with her as a memento. Before saying goodbye to Minoo and her father, I went to the mirror to adjust my scarf. As if I also had died so many years ago, I saw a tired, broken picture of myself in the mirror. I hugged Minoo, said goodbye, and left the old cob house, which looked like a mysterious ancient ruin in stories and films in which people search for treasure. After a few alleys, I saw the sign for "Social Security Office, Region 3" on the main street. I turned my face away. In front of me was the beautiful turquoise mosque. I thought about Sima's funeral. Probably when Minoo dies, they will wash and dress her in this mosque. Surely all the people of the town and even some from other cities and countries will come to her funeral. I know that when she dies, a huge number of people will see her off to her grave, talking in honor about this historical statue, which recently was distorted, and no one could repair, and even Mr. Hooshang will write a poem about her grief.

NAHID ARJOUNI

My Roots Were Somewhere with You

—*Translated from the Persian by Shohreh Laici*

Such a small world
you spend your days with the broken pieces of me,
fallen to earth.
I delete the borders from the books, from my hairs, too;
Father said, "Cut it off."
He added, "Fuck the horses' whinnies, we don't belong to this country!
Don't you understand?"
I disturb the earth and spread some of my ancestors' soil near
the geraniums,
and throw more on the broken and ugly asphalt of the streets.
I throw it on the face of the child who calls Grandma "foreigner," laughing.
Father said, "It happens a lot when your roots are somewhere else,"
and then he stopped talking.
My roots were somewhere with you,
and only the strange horses loved my whinny, those who belong to no land.
I think of my roots at school, in my headscarf, while the smell of blood
in the national anthem
made me deeply sad!
I think it's the earth's stupidity which lets us break it into pieces, borders.
I think it's the politicians' stupidity that never lets soldiers in love fear
death in war.
Sometimes I think my teachers are dumb, those who believe war is holy
and that not wearing the hijab helps the enemy.
I open my ponytail in class and the horses shriek.

Father said, "Your roots were somewhere else," and I was thinking of you who are somewhere else.
You hate the blood,
the politicians, too, those who never let soldiers in love fear war.

Kitchen God

—Translated from the Persian by Shohreh Laici

Oh dear God who is always in the kitchen

reading the names of my pill bottles,

please stand back!

I must do the dishes

and cook something for lunch, while

talking with you.

No, no need to help me, No!

I can handle things on my own,

I should vacuum my living room

and I won't serve burnt food,

I will also answer the phone,

and should clean my picture frame, do you remember this photo?

I was a little baby girl in this one

and you were so generous to me,

I didn't take tranquilizers so often!

I could feel your anger after eating strawberries and falling asleep,

the day I was thirteen, those white bedsheets and my dreams . . .

sorry to be rude,

but you were jealous of my pockets, my girlish purse, and even my wooden

jewelry box.

Oh dear God who sits in my kitchen!

Now I'm a mature woman and

I don't hide the things in my pockets.

My purse lies open on the table,

and I take one tranquilizer every eight hours

and my doctor has given me a prescription: Do not think.

Oh, dear God, please pick up your feet.

I want to scrub the floor!

CKLARA MORADIAN

How Light Shines Through the Blue Vase on the Windowsill

The surprise medical emergency that followed the premature birth of my first child, which has engulfed the first year of his life, and upended / bewildered ours, has not revealed to me any profound revelations or epiphanies. There is no poetry or sentimentality in it for me, nothing rich has distilled from the desperation and depravations that have marked our sleepless nights, nothing living has sprouted from the terror of palpable death so nearby, nothing has catalyzed or crystalized from the pangs of early separation or the enduring of pain day after day—nothing that I could string into words on a page worth reading. It was not meaningless per se, but the meaning of such needless suffering is lost to me, as is my will to reckon with the losses that have accumulated in pandemic isolation. And how can I reckon with something so random? How can I reckon with something that might have been caused by a cosmic ray splitting two cells in the wrong direction sometime in week four of gestation? What I know is that his birth is the single most important event of my life and also the hardest and most terrible. To this day, I cannot trust my own moods. Between my legs sits a gaping wound, still. What I know to be true, a year later, is that his birth was an undoing, a disintegration, a totality of experience so intense that it eclipsed everything. We are all just now emerging from that shadow. For me, to become a mother meant to also experience near calamity and despair. What I know to be true is: my child is the greatest gift, and I will never / can never give birth again.

My son, Mîr, whose name means *the world* and *peace* in Russian (his father's mother tongue), but also *prince* in Kurdish (my birth language), whose name is the first three letters of the word *miracle* in English, whose conception and birth is a near impossibility that stuns us, has in his first year of life been cut open and sewn back together, prodded and poked more times than I can count. Mîr, the descendant of genocide survivors on both sides of his lineage, was forced to fight to stay alive in his first hour of life, and this fact makes me angry, resentful even, of all who have known such unearned ease. I am baffled and outraged by those who insist there was a reason for it all, some grand plan that will reveal itself to me in time. Mîr is smiling at me now from across the table as I write these words with tears coming down my face. He is unaware of and unencumbered by the weight of history that runs through him. Mîr, my teacher, a love incomparable to any other. Here he is, so incredibly beautiful, alive, lively, so full of joy that I am humbled. But for me, there has yet to come the type of distance from the carnage and violence of it all to be able to have a chronological tale to tell. Grief has warped and distorted time, memories, even reason into an incomprehensible word salad of medical terminology, a soup of shrieks and disorienting images of machines beeping in the middle of the night and surgeons rushing in the early morning hours. I am still trying to coax the atoms of my animal body to reorganize around togetherness rather than fear.

What I want to tell you about instead is the color blue. The story of my son existing on this earth is so intricately linked to this primal color that to tell you about one means to tell you about the other. Yes, I mean the ordinary blue on a sports T-shirt, but also the stunning shine of the ocean merging with the sky. I want to share with you what it means to first notice something that is just a color, then pay such keen attention to it for so long that the attention becomes a partiality, an obsession, an affinity, long enough to fall in love, long enough for that love to then become devotion, an undulating and oscillating quiet sort of faith. What I want to share with you instead are the gifts of a thousand days of adoration. A thousand meditations. Endless hours of worship. In the age of distraction, what does it mean to focus on the meaning of one color for a sustained period? I want to tell you about looking for God in a blue gum wrapper lying on the sidewalk or the distant outline of a recycling bin across the street and then finding sublimity in a blue lace wrapped around my lover's torso. I want to tell you about a color so mysterious, so beautiful that it hurts. A color that is, much like my son, nothing short of a miracle. And how can one love something so singular, so spectacular, so extraordinary without falling to pieces? How can one remain uninterrupted, unchanged, unmoved in the face of a miracle? I ask these questions as I watch my child eat a blueberry, a joy that seemed near impossible when he was born with some of his organs disconnected from each other.

My adolescence and young adulthood languished in a foggy haze of destructive depression. On my arms, I still bear the scars of what can approximately be described as a slow wreckage caused by displacement, forced exile and migration, and intergenerational trauma. I was haunted by the loss of language, the humiliation of assimilation, the rejection of my queer body, the erosion of identity, the yearning for homeland, a state, the need for bodily integrity, agency after having been violated. A refugee, I had been severed from home and from myself at such a developmentally critical age that I was adrift with little direction. Misery dragged on and I moved from one crisis to another. And some time in that decade, I stopped seeing most colors. The world transformed into a dull shade of brown and green and at times numb colorlessness. I do not mean this as a metaphor (though it applies), I mean to say I lost actual somatic color vision. Wildflowers, the bright sparkly dresses of childhood Nowruz ceremonies, became inaccessible to me, meaningless even. The sky and the ocean were the same color as matte mud. I lost touch with all things beautiful. Poetry was dead. A cavity opened where my heart once beat for the music of my homeland. There was nothing but mourning. And God knows I mourned. I was bereft, mourning my childhood friend who was dressed in a blue scarf when she was murdered in an honor killing. For months, I slept in my car and refused to even speak to my parents.

Thinking back, I don't know how I managed to reemerge from that abyss, but in time, colors came back to me, one after another, a gradual return, a gradual homecoming, and I took steps to rediscover and reclaim my losses. I stopped being preoccupied with the "Kurdish question," the question of identity. I stopped hiding my queerness. I stopped asking for permission to exist. I stopped asking if I deserved to exist. I stopped asking others to affirm my existence. I stopped insisting to whomever would listen that my people and I do in fact exist. I went back to school, I gradually healed my relationship with my parents, I stopped harming myself. But the color blue was the last color to arrive. Seeing it again meant my color vision had returned and with it came a new freedom. When blue finally appeared, it was as if I had been cured of a long shameful illness that had left scars in its wake. I love blue for being what it is, a conduit for divine light, in all its shades. Healing. I know now why, for centuries, blue has been seen as a holy color by so many cultures.

Almost one thousand days ago, I decided to make note of and record all the blue objects that came to me in my new apartment (my first home on my own) as a way of anchoring and thanking the world for simple reminders that I had survived to my thirties. When I started this project, I admit that I thought of it, first and foremost, as an aesthetic fascination, but over time, over long hours of delving into songs about the color blue, films with blue palettes, works of blue art, the chemical composition of blue pigments, writings on and about blue, poetry that felt blue or read blue, objects that either emanated or encapsulated blue, visiting blue places, blue buildings, blue cities, feeling "blue," wearing blue clothes, owning blue furniture, learning theories of blue, having deep conversations about blue, growing blue flowers, and more profoundly receiving the blue that was shared and gifted to me by friends, lovers, family, colleagues, clients, strangers from every corner of the world, it became something more. With time, this blue project began to tell a story of having seen the pit of not just darkness, but colorlessness, a state of numb emptiness, and having emerged alive, amid a blue sea, enchanted, looking up at a blue sky, and feeling free enough to laugh again, feel joy again, love again. This blue project became a ceaseless faith in the idea that if you pay enough attention to something, that if you commit to something long enough, you will find whatever it is you are looking for. At least for me, the path to spirituality was in noticing the purple blue bloom of the Jacaranda trees.

Because I was able to see blue again, and because blue allowed me to see beauty again, I found the love of my life. When color was absent from my life, I often hid from beautiful things. Or worse, I actively damaged or sabotaged beautiful experiences. Love, at least secure healthy love, was difficult to hold on to precisely because I believed I did not deserve beauty. Once I was out of my pit of despair, once I was able to see blue again, I allowed myself to be loved. On that first date, when the love of my life walked into a bar holding a book of poetry by Auden in his hands, I received him with open arms rather than turning away from him as I might have at a younger age. I received him with the same attention I give to blue flowers and blue paintings. When we first met, I asked him: "If you had to pick one shade of blue to describe your heart, which would you choose?" and he replied: "Prussian blue." Orally administered, Prussian blue—or chemical compound $Fe_7C_{18}N_{18}$—is an essential medicine, an antidote to heavy metal poisoning, so significant in fact that it is listed on WHO's List of Essential Medicines, critical for basic healthcare needs. Accidentally created as one of the first modern synthetic pigments, it has a long remarkable history in chemistry, art, literature, and letters exchanged between historical figures. Structurally complex and extremely insoluble, the variability of this blue's composition makes understanding this color a meditation. The day he mentioned to me that this was his shade, I could not have known then or predicted the full meaning of this revelation, but in the days since, I have come to marvel at it.

I don't know if either one of us knew that we had found each other, that we had found what we had been looking for. But now I see that I have so clearly been given everything I have ever wanted (an antidote to despair). What does it mean to have your needs actually met? What do you do with a blue like that? You choose it! In my early twenties, I used to find Nietzsche's idea of "Eternal Recurrence" damning. I was terrified of it. But last night, as we made love, I found my younger self baffling. I know that I would choose him/love him over and over again. I would do the entirety of my life over, all the traumas and pain, if it leads me to a path back to his shade of blue. To me, he is the most remarkable of all blue shades. He is my redemption, my peace, my safety, and respite. His embrace has been my quiet cocoon of warmth and creativity. Because of him, I have known what it means to feel secure attachment, to feel whole, to sit silently, not at war with myself or the world. I know love. I know care. And we came together to make Mîr, despite being told by multiple specialists that a biological child would be impossible for us. But unlike my relationship to blue, love is not a state of perpetual awe. And unlike my relationship to blue, loving has not been a constant reverence. For love is also a wounding where we have been wounded. Love is also slow ruptures and sometimes slow(er) repairs. Unlike blue, love requires forgiveness.

After our son's birth, in the chaos of the postpartum months and multiple hospitalizations, our love was threatened by small moments of inattentiveness, inadvertent acts of betrayal, excruciating loneliness, shame spirals, and sorrow. And certainly, blue has not brought me or us closer to lightness or light. It has not given me or us the ease I hoped would come by declaring it a life raft. I have suffered since. The world has suffered. I am exhausted by suffering all around us. My strong, steadfast, kind partner has suffered. My son knows suffering far greater than most people ever will. But blue has become an ontology, an ethic, a political praxis of radical vulnerability, softness, mutual care, generosity, reciprocity. And to have blue in my life means there is still the possibility of magic, poetry, heavenly love, unbound, unending, uncompromising. Having once known the brownish fields of my own helplessness, seeing blue now means other landscapes are possible, such as my husband and I growing old and sipping tea from a blue cup under a Magnolia bloom. Other landscapes like Mîr chasing after our dog Adorno Blue are possible. Tell me the world will not end before then.

I admit that there is nothing original in my blue project. History is full of writers and artists bewitched by blue. More than any other color, blue has transfixed, possessed, and inspired. Some of the most profound philosophical contemplations have been born out of an encounter with blue. I was not trying to be original. I simply accepted my assignment. The fact that blue is a returning theme in history does not diminish the fervor with which I have come to surrender myself to it. So, what have I learned after a thousand days of loving blue? What has come out of devoting myself, immersing myself, abandoning myself in one color? How has intentionally caring for something so much changed me? Loving blue has taught me that the world is both broken and beautiful. Moments after Mîr was born, before they knew about his congenital conditions, he was put to my breasts to feed, but his lips turned blue—the blue of death—and we nearly lost him. I am unable to unsee this scene. I am unable to unsee this blue. Motherhood is both the best and most terrifying thing that has happened to me. It is the ultimate dialect. Some days carrying these two truths is too much, it makes me feel as though I will burst into tiny specks of dust. Blue is in fact not just any one thing. I have been irrevocably and unrecognizably changed by it. Much like my inability to imagine my life without Mîr, I don't remember the days when blue was not a part of me. I have been saturated in one color for so long that I don't know how it would feel to be without it again. Spellbound.

Spirituality for me is found not in scripture but in repetition, rituals, the ordinary tasks of daily living, laps and laps across the water, meditation on one word, how it may be reconstructed to spell another, taking one step in front of another for miles, cutting the same fruit open every fall, wearing the same pair of blue earrings every Monday, reading a poem for breakfast every morning, undulating over/under my lover every night, year after year, with this rhythm that is his heart beating, over and over, next to mine. I concede, religiosity creates a chasm, a fissure between people. It alienates rather than brings about the union I seek, but I return to the idea of divine grace, time and again, only to say I have endured this past year's suffering by way of determined, persistent, intentional, stubborn repetition. I have survived by patiently loving and by praying to the color blue. By resisting entropy, by taking a stance, by looking at the most ordinary of objects, like a strand of blue string or a sign on the freeway pointing to a rest stop, as if they were signs from God.

For Mîr's first birthday, over thirty members of our family and friends gathered for the first time since the pandemic and all wore the color blue, a testament to survival. This is how my solitary journey of living through my young adulthood and making it to motherhood has now become a communal participatory practice of meaning making. Blue is a ministry of love, mercy in the shape of a watercolor painting handed to me as a gift, an offering. Blue is not ephemeral. Blue is not a phase or infatuation. Blue, like my longing for homeland, is a constant. Blue is a verb. Ancestral ritual. To think that I would one day be overtaken by another color is to mistake a heavenly song with noise. Here is what I know: given the choice, I would give up all the blue and poetry in the world for Mîr to never have to be cut open and hurt again and for me to remain next to my spouse peacefully asleep in old age.

LARENA AMIN

What I See in My Sleep, March Thirty

Pacing
stepping away from the dreaded motifs
of cold ex-lovers and loose teeth

I brace myself in the fictional wind
linking arms with a faceless friend
only to stumble upon
the architecture of a Dream

Raging
reaching the heavens
high ceilinged
peeling

Adorned with a mural of bygone kings
—their histories tangibly mythical, unreal—
on light brown brick

Thin
boxy and pronounced
She wouldn't live forever
but she looked like home

Hampstead-ian window frames
curtainless
expose a baroque living

Her bright interiors
shining on our awestruck faces below
As we break our necks to see
how loving, how wise
this building could be

This hybrid tower
of my Socialist Dreams

Larena Amin

To My Friend Who's Older Than Me

When you were younger were you ever sad for a long time?

Are we the same height?

Is it a messianic burden? To mentor someone who could potentially be great, or wind up young and dead.

Are you real for real?

I love you, Do I love you?

What do you feel, when you know you've taught me something?

What are you doing when you're not realising you're teaching me?

Have you had ancient visions too?

Beach holiday?

Or is it too soon?

BALSAM KARAM

Event Horizon

—Translated from the Swedish by Saskia Vogel

It could have been any year at all—above the wharf gates the blossoms of the chestnut trees once more flamed like lanterns in the spring, and a haze stole in across the shore and lifted a spatter of pink water to the sky.

The city stretched out flat and spent and, like other summers, allowed itself to be swept into a rhythm of breathing other than its own; the surge, white and foaming, lapped the sandy shore in time with the cruise ships and along the avenues the cafés were once more setting out their tables and opening their parasols. Yielding, the beach spread beneath the tourist's white feet shuffling between the dense stands laden with soap and whisky; tired and bored, the standkeepers stood smiling by their carefully stacked goods. This one? I'm practically giving these away, how many would you like?

This was where the mothers and then the children of the Outskirts used to go: here to the market where, in the shade of the trees lining the promenade, they'd spread out a towel and place on it crocheted washcloths in green and pink, long necklaces made from crushed china and colored glass, and one or two trivets made from the spare books, bottle caps, and metal lids. Madame, feel this— the softest cotton and linen, crocheted and dyed by hand. I'm practically giving these away, how many would you like?

At dawn, first the mothers and later the children too would mount the Outskirts' only broken bicycle in order to spend three days and two nights carefully spreading out the towel on the promenade on which to display the necklaces and washcloths.

As the third night drew near the mothers and children under the cover of night would cycle all the way back, and once at the foot of the mountain help carry the bicycle up the slope of the Outskirts and in among its homes. There all the other mothers would be waiting with tea and sugar—with bread, butter, and coffee if there was any—and with freshly laundered shirts for them to change into.

It was either very late at night or very early in the morning.

It was early enough for the children to be up, but far too late for them to want to be asleep, and just as the children continued their play—waiting, watching, and running to the slope to see if anyone was walking uphill—the rising sun was like a blue-green blaze over the crest and so the day began.

Yes, the children and sisters of the Outskirts waited for these homecomers and welcomed them with heated water and mangos found among the rubbish and cut into small pieces over the fire. Just as they'd washed off the city dust and wrapped towels around their bodies, the homecomers were fed the now-warm fruit, which they carefully took in their mouths and rolled under their tongues. They wouldn't have had a bite to eat for a day and a half, and hoped, after a good night's sleep, to have a little more to eat, here at home, here in the shadow of the mountain which rose black against the red afternoon sky and right beside the ditch that flowed rippling clucking brown and green past the houses of the Outskirts. Here, at home, embraced by their own, with tea steeped over the fire and next to the walls of the houses, toward which the morning sun worked its way, warming the corrugated metal walls and tarpaulins stretched between the houses.

Later, when the Outskirts had found a second bike to use, the mothers and children who either dragged their coolers fully stocked across the beach or displayed their necklaces along the promenade in the evenings would cycle into town together and there would be more of them to do the carrying there and back, more to pick fruit, milk cartons, and what sacks of onions there were out of the dumpsters, and more to band together when cars, windows rolled down, suddenly slowed and stopped right across the street.

∴

It could have been any year at all; autumn arrived later than usual, replacing winter, and the water lines were extended and the taps replaced in accordance with Milde's terms and conditions. In the morning the Outskirts waited to hear further news of Milde's impending spaceflight and thus sat down to eat what was there, clustering around Essa's handheld radio on full blast. Had she left yet? Where was she? Would she stop by for a visit first? Who was holding her captive? The mothers and children continued to congregate for months until news of Milde ceased, and Essa no longer got up in the morning and no one dared knock on the door asking to borrow that radio for a while. One morning the children who were waiting for Essa at school would refuse to keep putting up with having an absent teacher and trooped to her door. You have to come back mama Essa, it's enough now, the children would say, and on the mattress Essa would lift the tattered rag from her eyes and sit up.

∴

It was the year of the launch and of sleepless nights in the pool—meals and coffee breaks in the canteen of a spaceport and the body that either laid itself down at its own feet in resignation or stretched out on the floor, trying to remember.

Milde ate when she was supposed to and slept when she was supposed to—went for walks when she was supposed to and showered when she pleased.

The women Milde got to know at the spaceport and who every afternoon invited her for tea and cake in the staff room, nothing more than a kitchen with five broken chairs and a window cracked open onto the courtyard, kept telling her how admirable she was and how they wished her luck. Milde would look at them and say: I'm doing this for my sisters and for the sake of the Outskirts. So that, if only for once in my life, I may blend into a surrounding that resembles me, and to live once more in the hope that somewhere out there is a world that wishes me well, a world that wants me as part of it.

Sure, I can go to space and die, why not? I'd rather die in the depths of a black hole than wait around to be executed here, if you see what I mean. I'm doing this so that I can sit back and rest for once, no knife or metal lid hidden under my pillow, and so that, if only for a day, I won't have to look at those same white faces that wish me harm.

Sure, I can go to space and die, why not? I'd rather die there than continue to be of service here, if you see what I mean. I'm doing this for the sake of my sisters and for the Outskirts—for the children and the slope and the cats' yowling as soon as it's bedtime and the mist pressing against the roofs; I'm doing this for the sake of the washing lines and the wash buckets, and for every tap in every place where taps are rusting away but dammit if they aren't still in working order, do you see what I mean?

The women would put a hand on her shoulder, slide the coffee pot across the table and sit there nodding silently. They would hug her yet again when she got up to leave, and in the evenings they would bring her tea and cake. You shouldn't go to bed hungry, they'd say, and Milde would nod and say thank you.

The nights were longer in the spaceport than in prison, she didn't know why.

The body that for eleven years had been missing its left eye and both index fingers would inspect its broken nose in the mirror at night and run a hand across its collarbones. It would trace the stub of its index finger over deep scars on its arms, legs, and stomach, and slowly count them in the glow of the bathroom light, as if to then be able to set them aside.

The body would try to remember what the prison pit had smelled like and what the body looked like when, after eleven days, it was finally allowed to wash off the menstrual blood that had run down its thighs and caked like dark cuts across its calves and heels. Milde would try to remember how painful it was and how pain was measured in those days, according to what measure and why, and how come she no longer measured pain in the same way.

She remembered that the places of torture were connected to the buildings where the prisoners lay on a damp prison floor and placed their hands gone cold and stiff under their heads until they went numb and the numbness woke them.

On one such prison floor, across which the prisoners had crawled blindly in search of a corner in which to piss and shit, Milde had also curled up, legs pulled to her stomach, and tried to fall asleep, this she remembered.

The places of torture and where Milde was later woken by her numbing hands and sought out the corner where she'd pissed before so she could piss there again were just below this prison floor that she was crawling across, scraping her body against in the dark. She crawled to the wetness in the corner, squatted and wiped her hand on the wall for lack of clothing to wipe herself with.

It was in one of the rooms below that prison floor that she'd sat awake on a chair for five days and five nights and repeatedly asked to go to the toilet; she was menstruating.

Milde had said: I need to pee and I'm menstruating, let me go to the toilet.

The blood, a variable flow, had run out of her and dried, she had writhed in the chair and gotten nowhere.

When she'd finally peed herself, the guard uncuffed her, then undressed her and wiped the floor dark with urine and soiled dark red with her shirt and trousers frayed at the knees and hems.

The guard had then picked up the stained clothes and dressed Milde again, lifted her back on the chair and pressed her body now cold in the wet garments against the backrest, hands cuffed behind her.

After that, he'd only approach Milde in order to undress, wipe up, and dress her. Ever colder and more bruised she'd slide in and out of his grasp, again and again slipping down to the floor and staying there.

When the guard, after no telling how long, had come over to wipe up what she'd been holding in and which had flowed out of her loose and light brown, she'd screamed that she'd rather be naked, they could leave her as she was, let me freeze to death, don't dress me again, don't dress me again you bastard do you hear me, you make me sick, Milde had screamed before she was met in the mouth by the butt of a rifle and collapsed.

Later she'd woken to the stench of herself and then to the absence of all sound. That's what it was like to face the pits, and that's how all the sisters with whom she later shared a cell would remember it: They'd opened their eyes in the dark and had found nothing, closed and opened them once again and again, found nothing.

In the pits at first each was kept on her own, wounded fingers had searched their own faces from mouth to eye socket—pressing into their eyes wide open to make sure their eyes were there—then let their hands drop down once more.

The prisoners had uttered something, to test their voice, and heard nothing. They repeated what they said louder now, still nothing.

They'd stuck their fingers in their mouth and felt their tongue, counted their teeth, and wiggled their toes. They'd run their hands across the bridge of their nose, wondering if their nose had always been like this and if so for how long, stroked their hair, wondering if the taste of blood had always been so pungent and if so since when.

The prisoners had lain down to sleep on the damp prison floor and pressed their noses to it, trying to sniff out the source of the damp and whether the wastewater was flowing down the rough walls; they'd wondered if someone else had been in here before them and if so who, and whether they were still bleeding menstrual blood or if the blood was coming from elsewhere.

Milde recalled that only when the cell door had been opened and something tossed in—first bread, then bottles of water hitting her body—did she realize her eyesight was still somewhat intact.

After that she'd searched for that chink of the door for days on end—crawling up to the door right when it was time for it to be flung open—and aided by the light tried to find what gave shape to her gaze and allowed it to navigate.

The prisoners had always shut their eyes at first, thus holding the memory of the chink of the door for longer inside them, bringing it to life between its opening, trying to imagine that somewhere out there was still a sky and a sun, a sandy beach, a sea, and cats scampering along the paths cut by mothers and children who fell into each other's arms and did not wish each other harm.

In time they learned to turn away from the door right as the key was shoved into the lock so as to let the light reveal to them something of their cell's interior; the floor and the ceiling, how small they were, the corners and the cracks, what was there.

The prisoners had let the light from the chink of the door illuminate the cell and then knew where to go to eat and where to pee—where to stay so the water bottles wouldn't hit their backs and chests, and where to lie down to sleep when nothing but sleep could help.

Milde recalled that in the places of torture the light would sometimes be tinged blue and sometimes be a dazzling white that knocked out her eyes now used to the dark. Later she was unable to conjure up the image of any other light as clearly and on some nights, still blinded, had difficulty sleeping. When one afternoon between coffees she told the women in the spaceport about this shifting light, each one created a memory of her own to bind to it. One said the morning my mother left me on my own and the other said when I was seven years old and got lost in the rooms of the hospital where my grandmother was on her deathbed.

Milde said: The torture room had a marble floor, gray and white concrete walls, and a steel chair that made the body conduct electricity.

She remembered that her body had been damp the whole time and that she'd fallen to the floor many times. She also remembered the interrogations and her back-bound hands, how the policemen would inhale, a cigarette between their lips, and blow smoke in the prisoners' faces, stamping lit cigarettes on the prisoners' nipples then forcing them to scrub their wounds clean with soap and water.

It was said that Milde was the brains behind the uprising, the first to suggest arson and the one who had long been agitating the children and mothers of the Outskirts; she'd been spotted at the scene and was said to be the one who'd procured the rifles and who refused to name her conspirators. This is why they'd stubbed out a cigarette in her eye right before the end of the final interrogation and she was carried to a cell where twenty new sisters were waiting and dropped among them unconscious. She was forced to remove the cigarette herself and after twelve days the whole eye with only a pair of nail scissors that someone had managed to smuggle in, afterward she didn't know what to do with the eye and finally summoned the guard and placed the eye in his palm. The sisters in the cell had clamped her head between their arms, pressed down on her chest as if to make her hold her breath and handed her the nail scissors with care. Milde had in fact held her breath and then collapsed, her hair was caressed slowly and softly and she stayed with her newfound sisters for eleven years.

In line at the spaceport's canteen, tray in hand, Milde would look at one of the servers and say: Once I ran across the mountain with a rifle over my shoulder and at dinner time my foot slipped and I fell into a hollow. It wasn't high up, but I was stuck there for hours while the sun was lapping at the sugarcane fields and stinging my eyes. Do you know how that feels?

Milde would say: In prison, I found a second home with other sisters and other mothers, and when they called me to solitary confinement, someone else always stood up and said, "Here I am" and followed the guard out. And they threw Sabina in solitary and they threw Marisol in solitary and they threw Silvia in solitary again and again. And one day when they called Sabina to solitary confinement, I stood up and said that I was her and gladly followed the guard who didn't notice that my left eye and both index fingers were missing. Do you know how that feels?

MERAL ŞİMŞEK

I Was Woman

—Translated from the Turkish by Burhan Sönmez

My anger started in the pages of the Torah

I've fallen in layers

from the verses of the Bible

I blew the Quran

In the question of my childhood

The braid of my hair was driven from Jerusalem to the Kaaba

My children were shot at the foot of my sadness

In a different color every century

From your religions to your gods

Crucified the white of my milk

I'm blessed in the sum of the misconceptions

I was shot while being blessed

My smile was stoned to death

However, in the invocation of my fingers, with an undated creation

The talisman of existence has incarnated

I died with what I created

I was a woman

I was multitude

I was not

Dream and Reality

—Translated from the Turkish by Öykü Tekten

clean tables were set

when the sun was scorched

bread was a stranger to our country

just as othering ourselves,

we burned and scattered our dreams

and sterilized all hopes

our refugee hearts turned to the loop of night

while the gods bore bastard seeds

in crimson gardens of paradise

we were banned from life, from falling in love

it was the time of laughter in thyme

each of us shouldered, one by one,

uncontainable weary dreams

we fell silent in orphaned solitudes

surrendered ourselves so that the world

would be a better place

in fact, we massacred ourselves

for a worthy life through slimy consolations

history of our consciousness filled with delusions

nothing more than a chain of silenced paradoxes

unanswered questions resided with our stagnation

blaming each sin on the darkness

as they became our biggest unanswered question

was it our dream that was the reality

or our reality, the dream?

HOLLY MASON BADRA

Waiting

Winter branches
silhouette

the darkening sky.
In trying to be tender,

I slice a pear
and add cinnamon.

The gate swings on a hinge.
Imagine

a crescent moon:
the beloved's ear.

And in her
eye

a silhouette
of winter branches.

Qurban

The adults would say it to the kids, *Qurban*.
Like the sound a sheep makes, it goes "Core-baan."

Qurban-e-bim, Kurdish translated into English means:
I am willing to sacrifice myself for you. I sacrifice myself to you.

A table of twelve chairs filled with aunts and uncles playing cards—
A young girl, I come up to my mother and whisper something into her ear,

I hear her tell them the secret as I walk away;
I hear them say, *Qurban*.

Not knowing then just what it meant, but knowing it made me feel
Both pleased and embarrassed—*Qurban*.

And now, when my own nephew is soft in my arms,
Opening his little hand to the early moon, saying "hold you, hold you,"

I look at him and the thing in my chest is *Qurban*.
Escaping my lips, *Qurban*.

HERO KURDA

Except for Poetry, Nothing Else Shields Me

The start of all biographical writing is strange and difficult. It is always difficult for me to talk about myself or how I fell in love with poetry. I would rather talk about something else than this short experience I have with poetry, but I am not completely against it. I accepted this request for a self-writing project from the beautiful writer Houzan Mahmoud, and so I will tell my simple story.

In our household, which consisted of my parents and four children, there were no other books besides those we had from school, not even a Quran. In 2004, we became the owners of a Quran which my mother kissed, put up on a shelf and said, 'I hope a day will come that you will read this book and not imprison it.' At that time, I had only been reading for a month or two. Hearing my mother say that taught me that an unread book is an imprisoned book.

Ever since I was a child, I have loved books. Kurdish books especially gave me a different feeling. I would ask myself how Kakay Falah could write like that or who helped Latif Halmat to write so beautifully about snow. With my tiny head, I always arrived at the conclusion that God had specifically chosen these men to write such beautiful poetry. This is because back then and even now, in all the examples of poets that exist in Kurdish school curriculums, one cannot find a single female poet. This made me believe that writing poetry was a man's skill. This was the time of the civil war.

We had been displaced from Kirkuk to a small town between Erbil and Mosul. It was a frightening time. Men listened to radios and women held their hands over their mouths and only repeated what the men said. All we ever heard was a long *shhhhh*. We did not understand what was happening, but we were afraid and understood that the men's gathering was not without concern. During this time, the school where I was a student (I don't remember its name) was turned into an office for the Kurdistan Democratic Party. On the wall of the school, some-one had written Long Live Barzani with a huge brush. I did not understand any-thing. We were transferred to another school building where we finished elemen-tary school, middle school, and high school. On Thursdays, I was afraid when we read poetry in class. The high school kids were much older than we were. When we were asked to read poems, the older boys and girls laughed at us and called us chicks. I had so often been called a chick that I associated being a chick with poetry. I told myself that as long as I read poetry, I was a chick.

In 2001, when I was only twelve years old, I lost my father, who was my closest friend and best supporter. I was so shocked that I could not express myself by talking about my pain and anger. I began writing poems without knowing anything about writing a poem, without having any kind of background or even an introduction. I wrote six poems about my father, on death, on loneliness, and other subjects along these lines. I was shocked at my own use of poetry; it began to feel like a game that was now in my hands. In a short period of time, I filled up a one-hundred-page notebook. I was almost annoyed by it; I wrote a poem on just about anything.

In 2003, on the second day of Kirkuk's liberation, we took a pickup truck and went back to the city. It was lost in smoke, the smell of asphalt, and burnt, black oil. I was fourteen years old and afraid. People were anxious; they ran, they laughed, they talked, they were very happy, but I was very afraid. My mother was among those who were very happy because, through all those years, she had only had one dream: to return to Kirkuk. I dreamed in my mother's dream; I recognised the city when my mother laughed. Whenever we drove from Erbil back to Kirkuk and saw the oil in the Shoraw neighbourhood, my mother would say, 'May I be sacrificed for your land and water, Kirkuk.' Although there has been terror, ISIS, and the troubles of party politics in Kirkuk, I still love the burning fire as before and have never hated this city even for a second.

When the smoke calmed down, there were openings for many media outlets—magazines, newspapers, and dozens of extracurricular activities. From 2004 to 2014, Kirkuk lived its golden years in terms of services provided for literary centres and art galleries. I published my work in many different magazines, for example in *Nawshafaq*, *Gizing*, *New Kirkuk Newspaper*, *Kirkuk Today*, *Kirkuk Tomorrow*, *Basara*, *Hawal* and many others.

My poetry continued to slowly improve until I was in ninth grade, when I timidly introduced my poems to my Kurdish teacher, Abdulrahim Sararo, who was also a poet. He said he would get back to me. I became so nervous that I had shown such nonsense to someone, and I regretted my choice a thousand times that night. Up until that point, only my family and relatives had read my poems. The day after, the teacher sent someone to call me, but I became so nervous I could not even carry my own weight. I would have rather died than see him make fun of me.

He welcomed me with an honest smile and immediately said, 'How are you, my daughter?' He did not allow me to answer anything with my shaky voice before he added, 'Your poems are beautiful. They are true poems; we only need to edit them a little bit. For example, this poem [I don't remember which poem it was] is a good poem and I plan to publish it this week.' He took out a piece of paper and told me to read some of the other poems and wrote notes for me. He looked at my forehead and said, 'You are a poet.' He made me the happiest person alive with just a few words in those brief moments.

I read the paper he gave me and kept it for several years. In it he wrote that I was a poet, that my poems were good and that he had shown some of my poems to other people, and they had also agreed with him. He said that I needed to read more, especially poems written by women. He wrote the names of a couple of women poets whose work he suggested I read.

That night, I could not sleep from all the joy I felt. Later that same night, when I realised regular reading was requisite to becoming a good poet, I felt sad because there was not a single book in our house. We also did not have the money to buy any books. My teacher took up that burden and would always bring me books, magazines and newspapers. Two days after I spoke to him, my poems were published, and everyone in the school saw them. From that day on, my life took a different direction. This was the end of 2004.

In 2005, there was a poetry festival for the youth in Kirkuk organised by the Centre for Youth, and I participated. Everyone looked older and more mature than me; I was only sixteen, petite and frightened, and in this state, I read my poem on stage. I was crying in my heart, and I kept telling myself that I was not capable. When I finished reading the poem, though, hundreds of people clapped for me in the audience at Shahid Sirwan Talabani Hall, and I quickly ran to my mother to hide myself. The cameras made me both nervous and excited. I was given an award, and then I performed another reading. Then another one. And another one. All of a sudden, it was as though I had become Hero Kurda, and everyone was supporting me and encouraging me to persist in my writing.

Afterwards, Khalid Kawesi taught me how to write speeches. He introduced me to journalism, and I became the tiniest feminist journalist and human rights activist. I was awarded a golden necklace from Kurdish organisations along with Human Rights Watch.

Day after day, the task became more difficult. I became dissatisfied with my own poetry because I started reading poems from around the world, including Kurdish and Arabic ones. I stopped seeing myself as a poet. I ripped up my poems and started writing again in a different style, but I did not like those either, so I just wrote and tore up my writing. I felt like I had reached a dead end, like I had lost my abilities as a poet and had ended up in a war where I could see my dead body covered in blood but was unable to do anything about it.

I took a break for a while and then started reading again. I came to believe that I was no longer able to write poems and that I had not had any talent in the first place. After a long period of continuous reading, I started writing again. I noticed a difference in my poems, and I was happy with it. I saw that I was able to be proud of myself and that there was a fountain of inspiration springing from me that was beautiful.

Participating in poetry readings and festivals and later studying linguistics and Kurdish literature at the University of Kirkuk introduced me to further literary works. It made poetry into a mysterious game of sorts; there was always something to discover and learn. The head of our department and all my teachers always encouraged me and were proud of me.

When I turned eighteen, I published my first poetry collection with my own money. At that time, I was content with the quality and so were my readers. Today, however, that book, which was titled *Burning in the Season of Flight*, does not make me or its readers happy.

Another battle with poetry had begun. I stopped writing once more, and only focused on reading. Then I began writing in a completely different style. For the first time, in 2010, I wrote an erotic feminist poem entitled 'Getting Naked.' During that time, I wrote mostly erotic poems. In 2013, I published my second collection entitled *I Write Joseph*. Most of the poems from that collection are erotic, and I love them as much as I would love my child because they are the products of my wounds. Later, eroticism as a concept became even more interesting for me, and in 2017, I wrote my master's thesis on women's erotic poetry in Southern Kurdistan.

Sometimes people ask me how it was that I could write erotic poems and not encounter trouble, or how I was not stopped from doing it altogether. Poetry inhabits its own strange realm. The impossible becomes possible and it makes one accept that which cannot be accepted and helps one find beauty in it. It is true that Kirkuk is going through its own special circumstances, but it is less influenced by what the mullahs have to say. The city has a centuries-old history of intellectualism and culture. Literature and culture are more dominant than oppression and prohibition.

After the war with ISIS and the events of 16 October and the fall of Kirkuk, writers and poets disappeared and these sorts of opportunities were fewer, but culture did not die out altogether. This is because a city that has a rich, centuries-old cultural and literary legacy and owns several publishing houses and galleries does not lose all its culture in such a short period of time. After a year and some months, literary activities, movie premieres, theatre plays and literary conferences started once again, with a high participation. The situation now is better, and people are hopeful that it will continue to improve, because literature is like air—one cannot easily abandon it.

My life in this city has introduced me to the public, and I was welcomed on TV and news outlets. Since there are few women writers in Kirkuk, my texts were easily introduced to different ethnic minorities, especially to Arabs, through translation. My poems have been translated a couple of times into Arabic.

The process of writing—since I was twelve years old until now, at age thirty—has always been a difficult and rewarding one. When writing poetry, I always alternate between long breaks and periods in which I continuously write. Except for poetry, nothing else shields me in this city, a city flooded with so many different religions, cultures, fire and war.

Acknowledgments

To all of the writers in this book, I cannot thank you enough for trusting me with your work! Thank you for your patience and vulnerability. Thank you for your kindness and care. You surrounded me with protection in pregnancy and postpartum. You've fed and nourished me in mind, body, and spirit.

A big *thank you* to the University of Arkansas Press team for midwifing this book into the world—Charlie Shields, Janet Foxman, Rachel Walther, William Clift, David Manuel Cajias Calvet. David Scott, thank you for the early conversations and continued feedback on this project. I am grateful for your support and encouragement (both in this book and in my new job title: parent).

This book truly wouldn't exist without some key figures in my life.

To my wife, Dani Badra, who has been my biggest cheerleader in this process and has always made me feel incredibly understood in my hyphenated Kurdish identity, I am so grateful for you, *hanasakam*.

To my mother, Hewi, and my big, loud Kurdish family, the Khoshnaws, thank you for instilling and fostering in us Kurdish pride and joy. Mom, *dayah*, thank you for sharing all your stories and influencing my love of storytelling. To Amineh (our BeBe), we've named our children after you—may they embody your strength, unwavering generosity, and good sense of humor. To my cousins, thank you for filling every space with laughter and for holding me through the tears. You are the greatest gifts a Kurd could ask for.

To my brothers, I've erased every sentence I've tried to type here because there is no way I can truly capture the gratitude I have for you two being who you are in my life. One of my poems in this collection is written while holding Smith. But the baby in that poem is also Vera, Thad, and Hannigan—all of my *qurbans*. To my dad, I wrote one of my first pieces of creative writing on your work stationery, sitting outside of your office. Thank you for teaching us to treasure creativity, art, music, and a good dance party.

Thank you to Hayan Charara for the phone conversation many years ago (with dirt still on your hands from tending to your yard) when you helped me believe that I could and should do this.

To my MFA creative writing family at George Mason University, who showed excitement for this collection, thank you. To Angela Barajas, thank you for your wisdom and thoughtfulness on the introduction. To Anu Aneja for your encouragement and enthusiasm about this work, I appreciate you, and to my other Women and Gender Studies faculty and colleagues, thank you for generating fruitful spaces and conditions for this work to breathe.

To the brilliant scholars running the Kurdish Student Organization at GMU, thank you for all the work you do to help spread an understanding and awareness of Kurdish culture and to help Kurds on campus find community and belonging. I value your presence in my life. Thank you for all your coalition building supporting Palestinian and other SWANA student groups.

Last and not at all least, to Iris, our tiniest Kurd, I love you, *qurbanibim*.

Credits

Many of these works have previously appeared in journals or are selected from published books. Some works appeared first in a journal and are now a part of a fuller collection. You can find these works in the following places where they were published before this anthology:

"Broken Ghazal with Words" and "In Another Dream Where My Father Apologizes" by Hajjar Baban in *Ruminate Magazine*, no. 57 (2020)

"Yesterday" and "A Night with No Country" by Zhawen Shali (translated by Arash Saleh and Holly Mason Badra) in *Circumference Magazine* (2022)

Excerpts from *Daughters of Smoke and Fire* by Ava Homa (Abrams, 2020)

"Object Exercise" and "Jin-Jiyan-Azadî" by Tracy Fuad in *about:blank* (University of Pittsburgh Press, 2021)

"Question" and "When I Dream About You" by Jîla Huseynî (translated by Farangis Ghaderi and Rinat Harel) in *Women's Voices from Kurdistan: A Selection of Kurdish Poetry* (Transnational Press London, 2021)

Excerpts from *Take What You Can Carry* by Gian Sardar (Lake Union Publishing, 2021)

"Secrets of the Snow" and "A Poet Was Murdered" by Hiva Panahi in *Secrets of the Snow* (Hard Ball Press, 2016)

"The Explorer Who Watched from a School Window" by Bayan Nasih in *Kurdish Women's Stories*, edited by Houzan Mahmoud (Pluto Press, 2021)

"Last Light" and "Tasseography" by Leila Lois in *Flesh into Blossom* (Published by the author, 2021)

"The War Was Over" and "A Child's Painting" by Nazand Begikhani in *Bells of Speech* (Ambit Books, 2007)

Excerpt from *Whispering Walls* (version altered in the novel) by Choman Hardi (Afsana Press, 2023)

"Family Rashomon" by Meryem Rabia Uzumcu in *Jasūr Magazine* (2021)

Pages from *Between Two Rivers* by Rooz Mohammed (translated by Halo Fariq and Hannah Fox) (KANO Print House, 2021)

"Setar on the Mud Wall" by Essmat Sophie in *Last Day of Autumn* (Transnational Press London, 2021)

"My Roots Were Somewhere with You" and "Kitchen God" by Nahid Arjouni (translated by Shohreh Laici) in *Two Lines Press*, no. 29 (2018)

"How Light Shines Through the Blue Vase on the Windowsill" by Cklara Moradian in *So to Speak* 32 (Spring 2023)

"Event Horizon" by Balsam Karam (translated by Saskia Vogel) in *Words Without Borders* (2019, early version co-translated with Alice Olsson)

"Dream and Reality" by Meral Şimşek (translated by Öykü Tekten) in *The Markaz Review* (2022)

"Qurban" by Holly Mason Badra in *The Northern Virginia Review* 31 (2017, originally published as "Kourban") and "Waiting" in *Bethesda Magazine* (2018)

"Except for Poetry, Nothing Else Shields Me" by Hero Kurda in *Kurdish Women's Stories*, edited by Houzan Mahmoud (Pluto Press, 2021)

Build Your Bookshelf

In addition to reading more from the writers in this collection, I want to point you toward further essential reading and collections amplifying Kurdish women's voices:

Kurdish Women Through History, Culture, and Resistance by Shahrzad Mojab (Mazda Publishers, 2024)

The Kurdish Women's Freedom Movement: Gender, Body Politics, and Militant Femininities by Isabel Käser (Cambridge University Press, 2023)

The Kurdish Women's Movement: History, Theory, Practice by Dilar Dirik (Pluto Press, 2022)

Kurdish Women's Stories, edited by Houzan Mahmoud (Pluto Press, 2021)

The Mother, The Politician, and The Guerrilla: Women's Political Imagination in the Kurdish Movement by Nazan Üstündağ (Fordham University Press, 2023)

The Purple Color of Kurdish Politics: Women Politicians Write from Prison, edited by Gültan Kişanak, prepared for publication by Ruken Isik, Emek Ergun, and Janet Biehl (Pluto Press, 2022)

Voices That Matter: Kurdish Women at the Limits of Representation in Contemporary Turkey by Marlene Schäfers (University of Chicago Press, 2023)

Women of Kurdistan: A Historical and Bibliographic Study (Society and Politics) by Shahrzad Mojab and Amir Hassanpour (Transnational Press London, 2021)

Women's Voices from Kurdistan: A Selection of Kurdish Poetry, edited by Farangis Ghaderi, Clémence Scalbert Yücel, and Yaser Hassan Ali (Transnational Press London, 2021)

Finally, a new Kurdish-owned press, Henar Press, dedicated to publishing Kurdish literature and translation, offers a comprehensive online database of Kurdish literature available in English. Visit Henarpress.org and select the "Kurdish Literature Database."

Contributors

Larena Amin is a London-raised poet and artist. Overarching themes in their work blend and amalgamate, bouncing off a clear foundation of ancient history, social cultures, and one's inner dialogue. A manual approach is pronounced in Amin's expression and production, gently embedding her artistic contribution into the local tapestries she traverses.

Nahid Arjouni's poetry is well-known for its exploration of femininity and war in the Middle East. She holds a master's degree in psychology and lives in Sanandaj, in the Kurdistan region of Iran. She has released three poetry books, published in Iran and Arbil, Iraq.

Hajjar Baban is a Pakistan-born Afghan Kurdish poet.

Holly Mason Badra received her MFA in poetry from George Mason University, where she is currently the associate director of the Women and Gender Studies program. Her poetry, essays, reviews, and interviews have appeared in *Meridian Magazine*, *The Arkansas International*, *The Adroit Journal*, *The Northern Virginia Review*, *Foothill Poetry Journal*, *The Rumpus*, *CALYX*, *So to Speak*, *Circumference Magazine*, *Asymptote Journal*, and elsewhere. She has been a panelist for OutWrite, RAWIFest, and Al-Mutanabbi Street Starts Here as a Kurdish American poet. Mason Badra reads for *Poetry Daily*.

Nazand Begikhani was born in Southern Kurdistan. She has an MA and a PhD in comparative literature from the Sorbonne. She has published ten poetry collections in Kurdish, English, and French. Her poetry has been published In the *Poetry Review*, *Modern Poetry in Translation*, *Poetry Salzburg Review*, *Poetry Action*, and *Ambit*. Her work has been published in French, Arabic, Persian, and English. She is a polyglot and has translated Baudelaire and T. S. Eliot into Kurdish. She has been editor of the Kurdish edition of *Le Monde diplomatique*, and is a dedicated advocate for women's human rights. She is a visiting professor at Paris' grande école Sciences Po, where she teaches "Methodological and Ethical Principles of Researching SGBV" in conflict zones and among war-affected populations. For her writing and activism against social injustice and inequality, she was awarded the Emma Humphreys Memorial Prize (Centre for Women's Justice, UK) and Kurdistan Gender Equality Prize.

Halo Fariq was born and raised in Slemani, Kurdistan, where he currently serves as a major with the Peshmerga, the armed forces of Iraqi Kurdistan. In his spare time he is an avid translator, and he has translated more than thirty novels into Kurdish, including Yoko Ogawa's *The Memory Police* and Haruki Murakami's *After the Quake*. His poetry translations have been featured in literary journals including *World Literature Today* and *Asymptote*. He is the cofounder of Nawendi Befr, a publishing house dedicated to translating children's stories and educational books.

Hannah Fox is a PhD student at the University of Leeds, UK. Her research focuses on literary representations of bibliomigrancy and censorship in twenty-first century world literature. She has co-translated various short stories and poems from Kurdish, with her work appearing in *The Markaz Review and Rusted Radishes*.

Tracy Fuad's second collection, *PORTAL*, won the Phoenix Emerging Poet Book Prize and was published in 2024 by the University of Chicago Press. A 2023 National Endowment for the Arts fellow, she is also the author of *DAD DAD DAD DAD DAD DAD DAD* (2019), *Pith* (2020), and *about:blank* (2021), which won the Donald Hall Prize. Her work has also appeared in the *Paris Review*, *Poetry Magazine*, and the *Best New Poets Anthology*. She lives in Berlin, where she teaches poetry and directs the Berlin Writers' Workshop.

Dr. Farangis Ghaderi is a lecturer in Kurdish and gender studies and the director of the Centre for Kurdish Studies at the Institute of Arab & Islamic Studies of the University of Exeter. She is the coeditor of *Women's Voices from Kurdistan* (2021) and has written extensively on Kurdish women, Kurdish culture, poetry, translation, and literary history. She is the principal investigator of the Kurdish Digital Archive project at the University of Exeter. Dr. Ghaderi is associate editor of *Kurdish Studies Journal* and also a literary translator.

Choman Hardi is an educator and author of critically acclaimed books in literature, academia, and translation. Poems from her first English collection, *Life for Us* (Bloodaxe, 2004) have been studied by secondary school students as part of their English GCSE curriculum in the UK. Her second collection, *Considering the Women* (Bloodaxe, 2015), was given a recommendation by the Poetry Book Society and shortlisted for the Forward Prize for Best Collection and translated into French in 2020. Her poems have also been translated into Italian. Funded by the Leverhulme Trust, her postdoctoral research, *Gendered Experiences of Genocide: Anfal Survivors in Kurdistan-Iraq* (Routledge, 2011), was named a UK Core Title by the Yankee Book Peddler. Her translation of Sherko Bekas's *Butterfly Valley* (ARC Publishing, 2018) won a PEN Translates Award. *Whispering Walls* (Afsana Press, 2023) is her debut novel. She is a recipient of the 2023 Franco-German Prize for Human Rights and Rule of Law.

Rinat Harel holds a bachelor's and master's degrees in fine art and studied creative writing at Emerson College, where she received the 2015 Writing, Literature & Publishing Graduate Writing Award in Nonfiction. Currently a PhD candidate in creative writing at the University of Exeter, UK, she is working on a collection of interlinked stories that revolve around life in Israel. Her poems and stories have been published in various literary magazines and won a few other awards. She also served as the translation-editor of *Women's Voices from Kurdistan: A Selection of Contemporary Kurdish Poetry*, published by Transnational Press London in 2021.

Maha Hassan is a Syrian-Kurdish novelist who, in 2000, was banned from publishing in Syria for her "morally condemnable" subject matter. She moved to Paris in 2004 due to threats against her and increasing pressure from the regime on Kurdish intellectuals. In 2005, the Human Rights Watch awarded her the Hellman/Hammett grant for persecuted writers. Hassan has been longlisted for the International Prize for Arabic Fiction twice (*Umbilical Cord*, 2011; *Female Voices*, 2015) and for the Sheikh Zayed Book Award three times (*Aleppo Metro*, 2017; *Good Morning, War!*, 2018; *The Neighborhood of Wonder*, 2020). She was also shortlisted for the Naguib Mahfouz Medal for Literature for *The Neighborhood of Wonder* in 2021. Her most recent novel, *Maqam al-Kurd*, was published in 2023 by almutawassit. She currently lives in Morlaix, France.

Ava Homa is an acclaimed author, speaker, and faculty member at California State University, Monterey Bay. Her debut novel, *Daughters of Smoke and Fire* (Abrams, 2020), secured a spot among the best books of the year in outlets like the *Wall Street Journal*, *The Independent* (UK), and *The Globe and Mail* (Canada). It was featured in Roxane Gay's book club, won the 2020 Nautilus Silver Book Award for Fiction, and was a 2022 William Saroyan International Prize for Writing finalist. Her collection of short stories, *Echoes from the Other Land*, was nominated for the 2011 Frank O'Connor International Short Story Award. Homa holds a master's degree in English and creative writing from the University of Windsor, and her essays and fiction have been published and anthologized across the UK, the US, and Canada. She has delivered speeches across Europe and North America, including at the United Nations in Geneva.

Jîla Huseynî was born in Saqez, Iran. Like many of her peers in Iran, she began her writing career by writing in Persian and teaching herself Kurdish. Her position at the Radio Sine (Sanandaj) gave her the opportunity to further develop her writing. She published her poems in literary journals and magazines such as *Sirwe*, and her first poetry collection, entitled *Geşey Evîn* [The blooming of love], was published in 1995. Her life was tragically cut short in a car accident at the age of thirty-two when she was on her way to meet the legendary Kurdish poet Sherko Bekas. Her *dîwan*, *Qellay Raz* [The fortress of mystery], was published posthumously in 1999 in three parts and included her Kurdish and Persian poems and as well as short stories.

Balsam Karam is of Kurdish ancestry and has lived in Sweden since she was a young child. She is an author, librarian, and university lecturer, and made her literary debut in 2018 with the critically acclaimed "Event Horizon," which was shortlisted for the Catapult Prize. *The Singularity* (Feminist Press, 2024) was shortlisted for the August Prize and is her first English-language publication.

Hero Kurda, also known as Hero Hisam Aldin, was born in Kirkuk in South Kurdistan. She started writing poetry for the first time in 2001, and was first published in 2004. Kurda lives in Kirkuk, where she works as a teacher.

Shohreh Laici is a US-based Iranian journalist, writer, and translator. Her essays and translations have appeared in a range of US journals, including *World Literature Today*, *The Brooklyn Rail*, *Michigan Quarterly Review*, *The Millions*, *Two Lines Journal*, *Asheville Poetry* Review, and many others. A documentary about her journey to America and fight for freedom of expression, entitled *My Room in Tehran Is Called America*, is currently in production by US filmmaker Pirooz Kalayeh.

Addie Leak is a translator and editor based in Amman, Jordan. She is co-translator of Mostafa Nissabouri's *For an Ineffable Metrics of the Desert* (2018) and Hisham Bustani's *Waking Up to My Distorted City* (2023), and her translations from French and Arabic have also been featured in *Souffles-Anfas: A Critical Anthology from the Moroccan Journal of Culture and Politics*, *Words Without Borders*, *The Common*, *The Georgia Review*, *Shuddhashar*, *Exchanges*, *The Huffington Post*, and more. She is a former Fulbrighter in Jordan, where she lived for six years and now lives again.

Leila Lois is a dancer, writer, and curator of Kurdish and Celtic origin who has lived most of her life in Aotearoa. Her poetry, stories, and essays have been published in journals and online in Australia, New Zealand, and internationally.

Rooz Mohammed lives in Slemani and studied graphic design at the College of Fine Arts–University of Sulaimani. She is the art and design officer at the non-profit Hiwa Foundation. She is the creator of the graphic novel *Between Two Rivers*, which was chosen and funded by Goethe-Institut's Spotlight Iraq project in 2020.

Shene Mohammed received her MFA in literary translation from the University of Iowa. She teaches literary translation and translates from and into Kurdish. She has worked as a director of the translation department at the Kurdistan Center for Arts Culture, and translator and assistant director at Kashkul, a research and arts collaborative. She worked as a managing editor for *Exchanges: Journal of Literary Translation*. Her writing has appeared in *World Literature Today*, *M-Dash*, *Modern Poetry in Translation*, *Poetry Magazine*, *Michigan Quarterly Review*, *Balinde*, and *Chirok*.

Cklara Moradian is a diaspora Kurd and former child refugee shaped by Kurdish liberation movements. She is now an independently licensed clinical social worker in California. She manages large-scale behavioral health projects and teaches graduate students at California State University, Northridge. Her psychotherapy and teaching praxis is rooted in anti-oppressive, anti-colonial, and liberatory frameworks. A burnt-out activist and aspiring writer, Moradian finds healing in indigenous Kurdish cultural practices, community building, and poetry. Her writing chronicles her journey with grief, displacement, and parenthood in a dying world. When she's not working, she can be found walking in botanical gardens or near a body or water with her loving spouse and beautiful child. She surrounds herself with the color blue to remember beauty in the face of an uncertain future.

Bayan Nasih was born in Hasar, a village outside the city of Kirkuk in South Kurdistan. She now lives in Sweden. She is a sociologist and expert in the Swedish national team for the prevention of honor-related crimes, forced marriage, and female genital mutilation. Nasih is a graduate from the University of Baghdad, with a degree in statistics. She also studied social work at Stockholm University. She is an activist defending the rights of women and children. She also writes poetry.

Dr. Hiva Panahi was born in Sanandaj, Iran. A young voice in Kurdish literature and philosophy, she received an award from the Mitterrand Foundation. She holds a PhD in political sociology from Panteion University, Greece. As an author and poet, she has been distinguished internationally for her contribution to Kurdish and classic studies. Her poetry has been included in various anthologies, including Karen Van Dyke's *Austerity Measures: The New Greek Poetry* (New York Review Books, 2017). Her poetry collection, *Secrets of Snow*, was published in 2001 in Kurdish, in Greek in 2008 (self-translated), and in English in 2016 (self-translated). In 2024, a selection of her three poetry collections with the title *Poetry of Light* was translated from English into Bengali by poet Dr. Rudra Kinsuk (Bhashalipi Publishing House). Dr. Panahi was racially persecuted by Greek extremists between 2011 and 2022; she left Greece and is based in Switzerland.

Narin Rostam is a Kurdish poet and journalist. She has been publishing her works since the age of fifteen and she is the author of two collections of poetry, *The Cardboard Hero* (2013) and *Upside Down* (2021). She earned her BA in theater production from the College of Fine Arts–Salahaddin University. She lives in Hewlêr, located in the Kurdish region of Iraq. Her new works have appeared in *Jineftin*.

Gian Sardar was born in Los Angeles. Her father is from the Kurdistan region of Iraq, and her mother is Belgian American from Minnesota. She studied creative writing at Loyola Marymount University, is the author of the novels *When the World Goes Quiet* (2024), *Take What You Can Carry* (2021), and *You Were Here* (2017), and is the coauthor of the memoir *Psychic Junkie* (2006). Sardar's work has appeared in the *New York Times*, *Confrontation Magazine*, and on Salon.com, among other places. She lives in Los Angeles with her husband and son, and she enjoys gardening, cooking, and other forms of procrastination.

Arash Saleh is a Kurdish activist who currently lives in the US. He was born in Eastern Kurdistan. He studied law in Iran and political science in the United States. He started his activities as a journalist in Sanandaj. He is currently involved in advocacy for the rights of Kurdish people.

Zhawen Shali is a Kurdish poet and journalist. She was born in Suleimani in Southern Kurdistan. She graduated from Sulaimani Polytechnic University and worked as a journalist for several Kurdish outlets. She published her first book, *The Autumn of My Life*, in 2008 (Sulaimani Pen House). Her second book, *Neither*

You Nor Rain Stayed, was published in 2013 by the Kurdish Writer's Union in Erbil. She has won several national and international prizes in literature. She currently lives in the US.

Meral Şimşek is a poet, novelist, and editor born in Amed (Diyarbakir) and is a member of Kurdish PEN and PEN Berlin. Her publications include the novel *Pomegranate Stain* (2017), the story "Arzela" (2022), and poetry collections *Refugee Dreams* (2013), *Clouds Raining on Fire* (2015), *Black Fig* (2017), *All Tribes – Nothingness*, and *German Feigenflecken*. Şimşek has received many literary awards, including the Theodor Kramer Prize, rewarding writers in resistance or exile, in Austria in 2022. Due to the content of her books and the awards she received, the Turkish government accused her of making propaganda. The prosecutor's office requested a prison sentence of up to thirty years. After a lengthy and tumultuous escape process from Turkey to Greece and back to Turkey, in July 2022, PEN Berlin managed to bring her safely to Germany, where she currently lives in exile.

Burhan Sönmez is the author of six novels. He is president of PEN International and a senior member of Hughes Hall College and Trinity College, University of Cambridge. His novels have been translated into forty-eight languages and received international prizes, including the EBRD Literature Prize and Vaclav Havel Library Foundation's Disturbing the Peace Award. He was born in Turkey and grew up speaking Turkish and Kurdish. He worked as a lawyer in Istanbul before going to Britain for political reasons and living there in exile for several years. He has been on the judging panel of several events, including the Inge Feltrinelli Prize and the Geneva International Film Festival, and has written for media outlets such as *La Repubblica*, *Der Spiegel*, and *The Guardian*. He has translated William Blake's poetry book *The Marriage of Heaven and Hell* into Turkish. Having written five novels in Turkish, he began to write in his mother tongue, Kurdish, with his most recent novel, *Lovers of Franz K* (2025). He lives between Cambridge and Istanbul.

Essmat Sophie (Asima) is an award-winning author, film director, researcher, translator, and activist. Born in the Kurdish region of Iran, she now resides in Norway after living in the United States. She holds master's degrees in English literature (University of Oslo), information science (University of Oslo, University of Tehran), and social science (University of Utah–Salt Lake City). Her notable works include *Dancing Amid Fire, Rising Above Ruins* (2023), *Last Day of Autumn* (2022), and *In the Eye of the Storm* (2013), which won Norway's Ordknappen Prize. As a filmmaker, her latest animation, inspired by her novel, won multiple international awards including those at the Cannes Film Awards, Female Eye Film Festival (Canada), Stockholm City and Vasteras Film Festival, European Short Awards, and the Toronto International Women Film Festival. Sophie has translated several works, including *Women's Journey from Shadow to Light* into Persian. She is a public speaker on women's rights, Kurdish issues, and human rights.

Öykü Tekten is a poet, translator, archivist, and editor. She is also a founding member of Pinsapo Press, an art and publishing experience with a particular focus on work in and about translation, and a contributing editor and archivist with Lost & Found: The CUNY Poetics Document Initiative. She is the co-translator of *Separated from the Sun* by İlhan Sami Çomak (Smokestack Books, 2022) and the translator of *Selected Poems* by Betül Dünder (Belladonna*, 2023). Her work has appeared in *American Poets Magazine*, *Poetry Magazine*, *Words Without Borders*, and *World Literature Today*, among other places. She is the general editor of Kurdish Poetry Series at Pinsapo Press, as well as the co-editor of the anthology *Best Literary Translations 2024* (Deep Vellum). She lives between Granada and New York.

Meryem Rabia Uzumcu is a graduate student worker at Rutgers University, where she is completing her PhD in women's, gender, and sexuality studies. She is thrilled that her audio story, "Family Rashomon," has furthered her relationships and work in Diyarbekir/Amed, a site critically situated in anti-assimilation and anti-colonial struggles internationally.

Saskia Vogel is the author of *Permission* (2019) and the translator of over twenty Swedish-language books. She was awarded the Berlin Senate Endowment for Non-German Literature and was a finalist for the PEN Translation Prize. She worked on *The Singularity* by Balsam Karam (2024) as part of her translation residency at Princeton University. Originally from Los Angeles, she now lives in Berlin.

Pınar Banu Yaşar is a Kurdish poet, with publications in various journals and anthologies. They are a Brett Elizabeth Jenkins Poetry Prize finalist, a Poetry Online Launch Prize finalist, and founded the Kurdish Poets Collective. Since 2019, they have received repeated support from the *Kenyon Review* and the Tin House Summer Workshop.

www.ingramcontent.com/pod-product-compliance
Lightning Source LLC
Chambersburg PA
CBHW031120020726
47495CB00007B/2274